I0823038

The Art of the Clash

JUGENDSTIL
Max Liebermann
THE ANATOMY OF COLOUR
LALLA ESSAYDI
KATY HESSEL
DÉCORS BARBARES
L'ART

SOPHIE VON OERTZEN WILLIAMSON
The Art of the Clash
A Manifesto Against Mundane Design
Gibbs Smith

Impressionism Phoebe Pool
Die Wohltat der Kunst
COLLECTING CONTEMPORARY
TASCHEN
KUNST des 20. Jahr-hunderts

To Mami. Thank you for being my biggest inspiration. I miss you every day.

And to Schatzi and my three monsters. You're my rocks.

Contents

Introd

uction

Making a House Your Home

How do you distill a concept so deeply rooted in your instincts that it feels like second nature? For years, I struggled to define my approach to interiors. When people would ask, "Is your style eclectic, maximalist, or traditional?" I'd often respond, "Whatever looks good?" with a shrug—a vague answer for something that defies easy classification. This partly stems from a deeply rooted imposter syndrome: I did not think I was a creative person, least of all a designer, until very recently.

But if I were to name it now, it would be *the art of the clash.*

The magic of design lies in transformation—what takes a room from ordinary to extraordinary, or as interior designer Beata Heuman so aptly says, "what makes a room sing."

What does the transformation entail? Where does it stem from? For me, it lies in the creation of tension, of contrasts, of ways to caress your eyes and your senses. This can be achieved in various different ways but the goal is always the same: to create magic. A space comes alive when it lets the eye wander, inviting you to linger and discover its layers. This is the heart of my design sensibility, what I call the art of the clash. It's not merely about opposites clashing, though. Finding the right balance can be an amazing exercise.

I sometimes compare the tension I crave in design and interiors to a chocolate chip cookie. Once you've tried a chocolate chip cookie sprinkled with some salt flakes, you will always notice when the salt is missing. A cookie without salt is still good, but one with salt is mind-blowingly good, all because of the tension of sweet and savory flavors touching all your taste buds. This explosion and caressing of the senses is what I want to achieve in every design I create, and what I want to help you create with this book. The fascination with contrasts is something I've carried through every aspect of life. Food as already mentioned—I love Thai cuisine with its complex flavors—but also fashion where I love nothing more than pairing a silk skirt with a work boot. I'm drawn to the tension that reflects the human experience in all its diversity. Perhaps it's my curiosity, or maybe it's a need to stand out. Whatever the reason, it's a thread that has woven itself through my life.

For years, I dismissed my creativity, thinking of myself as someone who could "put things together" but not as someone inherently creative. It took a life-changing period—having a third child, navigating a layoff, and confronting a personal crisis—to uncover a creative energy I didn't know I had. Since then, I can't imagine life without it. Once found, this creativity became a part of who I am.

My mother, who is one of my greatest influences, did not revel in the clash. Conversely, Mami loved to make everything match. Her outfits were always color coordinated, from shoes with matching bags to an impressive array of tights matching her skirts. The same could be said for her interiors. Her final apartment in Munich, where my family and I spent a year after she passed away, was an exercise not so much of constraint but rather of perfectly crafted spaces and vignettes. Her living space was an array of straight lines, a beautiful warm beige on the walls that were lined with contemporary art in black frames. One of my first changes when we moved in was to paint squiggly red lines around the windows. I couldn't bear the perfection of it all.

And this brings me to what made me a lover of imperfections, of contrast, of tension: my mother's need for absolute perfection. While everything was always extremely *gemütlich* (think hygge, but German), it was also always perfect. The extent of a mess Mami was able to create looks perfectly tidy compared to my explosive chaos. She always tidied up after my messes, though occasionally she would freak out and throw everything on the floor, demanding that I clean it up. But it never stuck, my piles and messes slowly gathering again throughout the house. To this day, I'm awfully unorganized and need to be very disciplined in order to make everything look as pretty and tidy as I want it to be.

Dearest Art Collector,
It has come to our attention that your collection, like most, does not contain enough art by women.
We know that you feel terrible about this and will rectify the situation immediately.
All our love,
Guerrilla Girls

Yet, with all her love of perfection, she was a welcoming and loving woman. Warm, laughing, hospitable, always being her own best guest, which was one of her mantras that we'll explore in Part Two. Nobody taught me more than Mami about how to make people feel welcome, at home, and just so relaxed they wouldn't want to leave. In fact, more than once, she would go to bed while the guests were still partying. Nobody minded, least of all she.

Another thing that has shaped my design philosophy is how my family is constantly moving. Over the fifteen odd years that my husband and I have been married, I've decorated nine of my own homes, evolving my style with each one. While these experiences didn't make me a better designer overnight, they helped me understand what works for me—and what doesn't. I understand how to create a home for my family, which lighting makes a room the coziest, and that not every color works in every room. I have learned that windows without treatments might look okay at first, but after installing the curtains, it's clear that the room resembled a face without eyebrows.

The hardest part in this is my impatience, which has led to a few design mistakes but also inspires a devil-may-care bravery. I like to *just do it*—be it a daring paint color or hanging a piece of art—because if I leave a decision too long, there is a risk we'll move again before I ever get around to actually doing it. Ever so rarely, I envy my friends who have a space they slowly develop and grow into. And then I remember how I absolutely adore my life and how I would never have discovered my explosive creativity had it not been for all the moving. Then I go back to just being extremely grateful for my life. And I look for something I can redesign, paint, or move, always looking for a new art-of-the-clash moment.

HOW TO USE THIS BOOK

A bit of housekeeping before we begin. The book is structured into two parts looking at what makes the art of the clash in a house. To illustrate my points, I'm showing you three of my own homes, both past and present: a rental flat in Klosters, Switzerland, a place that we call our home when we visit our families in Europe; a 1920 Tudor house in Shaker Heights, Ohio, that was my first foray into design; and New Canaan, Connecticut, our current home. Throughout, you will also find some photos of my childhood home, which was once photographed for a magazine. It's pure nineties style, and I treasure the images as a wonderful throwback and keepsake of my beloved Mami. You might also discover a few pieces of furniture that we have used throughout our other homes.

Also included are two gorgeous homes of friends that weren't designed by me but are prime examples of the art of the clash. One is Amanda Loehnis' gorgeous historical home, called Puddleduck Farm, that she updated with a keen eye to an overall style but with distinct vignettes that make you want to discover more. The other one is of my beloved friends, Hinrich and Wolfgang, who live in Hamburg.

PASTA ITALIANA

Their townhouse is unique not just because of its location in a grungier part of town but also for its commitment to antiques and warmth at the same time.

Part One then is all about the layers that I consider when creating the art of the clash, with helpful advice on how to start discovering your personal taste, the special sauce that will make your house a true home. Part Two takes a closer look at some of the specific spaces inside the home—bedrooms, kitchens, living rooms, and more—so you can think about how to achieve a splash of tension that works for you and how you live in those spaces.

With this, I invite you to join me on a journey to find your art of the clash. It feels different for each and every one of us—as it should! Whether you already embrace bold colors, audacious prints, and eclectic styles, or you're eager to introduce them into your life, this is a journey to help you create a home that feels distinctly yours. I hope to help you find your own unique mix and soul for your home; you are the one who needs to love it and live in it after all. Let's be inspired and create some magic together. ❖

PART ONE

Layers

The concept of layering took me a while to grasp. Not because I wasn't creating them but rather because it came so naturally to me—yet I lacked a clear understanding of the actual concept. My styling tended to be haphazard and not at all deliberate. Giving myself a structured framework helped direct my instincts for style and design. The end results were similar, but I arrived there faster, which is heaven sent when you're styling your ninth home in just fifteen years.

Layers are exactly what the name suggests: elements added to a space in different stages. They begin with foundational choices like paint or wallpaper, followed by furniture, soft furnishings (rugs, curtains), lighting, and artwork. The final touches are the small details—the cherries on top—that bring the space to life.

This order isn't rigid, of course. As inspiration can come from anywhere, there is a good chance that you stumble upon an item that determines the whole design long before you've even thought of the wall color. The most important takeaway is to prioritize what brings you joy. After all, it's your space, and it should reflect your tastes and preferences (perhaps with some input from your partner, but even that's debatable).

Looking back on our previous homes, and even my mother's beloved flat in Hamburg, a structured approach to layering could have helped certain spaces. While they were always inviting, they sometimes fell into the trap of being "pretty by familiarity." What I mean by that is, when you live with something long enough, you stop noticing its shortcomings. You grow accustomed to bare windows or the absence of a rug, overlooking how these elements could add to the space.

BEST

This awareness marks a key difference between a designer and someone who decorates as a hobby. Mastering the art of layering has been one of the most significant learning curves of my career.

The cherry-on-top layers are the real sign of a collector's mindset. And there is one piece of advice I willingly give any and everyone who wants to create a warm and cozy home, brimming with character and the art of the clash: say yes.

Say yes when a family member offers you an old trunk (like the one in our mudroom in New Canaan). Say yes when your parents are clearing out your childhood bedroom to make way for a home gym and need to offload your bed (like the one my son uses, passed down from my great-grandmother). Always say yes to art, knickknacks, textiles, or lamps. Essentially, embrace the potential in every piece.

Layering is both an art and a science. It's about more than filling a room; it's about creating a space that feels intentional, inviting, and uniquely yours. By embracing a structured yet flexible approach and cultivating a collector's mindset, you can transform your home into a space that makes it uniquely yours. ❖

Color Everywhere, or Why I Can't Stand White Walls

White spaces can evoke mixed emotions. For some, they are a classic; for others, they can feel uninspired. While I admire designers who create warm, inviting atmospheres using only white—a feat that requires a nuanced understanding of its many shades—I've come to accept that white spaces aren't for me. My own style leans toward the layered and the vibrant, driven by a love of color, pattern, and texture.

Nevertheless, white, when used strategically, is an essential tool in design. It creates tension and offsets bold colors, allowing them to sing. But a home filled solely with white rooms feels incomplete to me. I need vibrancy to thrive, and so my designs use white as a counterpoint rather than the main act.

Take, for instance, our flat in Klosters. The rental's all-white walls are uninspiring, typical of Swiss apartments with their textured, wood-chip wallpaper that's notoriously difficult to paint. Yet, by using as much art and textiles as possible as well as fairly large furniture, I was able to create a space that was welcoming and colorful. Proof that even in an all-white room, color and the art of the clash can prevail.

We also lived with white walls for five years during our years in Singapore. I never found the nerve to paint the rented condos we lived in, but it drove me crazy—although my husband may have suffered more due to my constant complaining. In hindsight, I should have just painted the rooms and been done with it, but I made the space work without colorful walls. It helped that Singapore is such a vibrant and colorful city. It was in Singapore that I discovered, one could even say *uncovered*, my creativity. The amalgamation of Chinese, Malay, Indian, and European cultures that cumulates in the ever colorful, ever tension-loving Peranakan culture meant that inspiration was around every corner.

Looking back, I grew up with colorful homes. It was the nineties, and yellow—especially earthy, soft, mustardy tones—were popular. My mother was also enamored with making spaces happy, so yellow was a must. Then a beautiful green for the walls of my grown-up bedroom at home. Our first rental flat in Luxembourg City as young married parents had an eggplant living room and a bright blue kitchen. Then a brown galley kitchen for our first house as official homeowners also in Luxembourg City, now with two kids, complete with a bright red living and dining room. (A lesson to always test colors before deciding to commit as the shade of red I chose was just too bright; especially at night it would bathe everything in a red glow.)

HERGÉ
COLORISATION
INÉDITE
TINTIN
EN
AMÉRIQUE

TOP Our chocolate-brown galley kitchen in Luxembourg. I created the bar seating to give us more space, with wall shelving and an armoire for storage. With the dark brown I didn't dare add another tone. Nowadays, I would have probably added some more colors to the brown and white mix. **LEFT** Even though this looks white, our office in Shaker Heights was actually painted in Morning Ritual by Backdrop, a warm greige. I love this shot because it shows so well that a color contrast can create a wonderful interest—in this case with the red office chair.

But how does one decide on a wall color? I can find inspiration anywhere, but I always look for the unusual, for a combination that isn't common. It's that tension that makes a space vibrate, makes your eye travel, and creates the atmosphere we crave. My preferred way to find said tension lies in nature. Think of a bird of paradise: its riot of saturated orange, acid yellow, electric blue, and glossy green sounds like a recipe for disaster, yet in the wild, it's nothing short of breathtaking. Those colors shouldn't sit together so comfortably—and yet they do. I have a whole folder on my phone with intense color combinations that scream tension—and I can't wait to use them in a project. Nature is full of examples of "bad taste," but we always love it.

Art is another, obvious, inspiration. My first real foray into what art can evoke in you was a children's picture book that I absolutely obsessed over as a child called *Linnea in Monet's Garden*. It's the story of a young girl who visits the Impressionist artist Claude Monet's gardens and re-tells Monet's story and her own in a scrapbook-like way. Not only did I learn all about Monet's life and way of working, it also

TOP View from the mudroom into the souterrain sitting room in New Canaan. A prime example of how to clash colors coherently: the grayish blue-green, Road to Todos Santos by Backdrop, is counteracted by the warm terracotta of the window wall, painted in Ghost Ranch by Backdrop. This combination is repeated on the first level of the house, where I used Ghost Ranch for the entry hall, staircase, and upstairs hallway. Road To Todos Santos starts in the back hall and continues to include the basement hall as well as this room. Without this balance, the green might have been overwhelming and given a feeling of being in an aquarium RIGHT Red and brown is a recurring theme throughout the flat in Klosters. While red is a primary color, it is complemented by the warmer tones of the brown and helps to lift the drabness of the white walls. Some dollops of dark greens and blues are also present throughout the apartment, adding to the coziness. It is a place in the Swiss Alps, after all.

gave me a fascination with his use of color. It should have been a bit of a giveaway that I love color and would work with color one day in my life. Monet is also a great example that trying and failing and trying again is part of every creative process. He is famous for the many canvases that he overpainted and started again. A reminder that we can't become a master if we don't dare to fail, and that you should just paint that wall—you can always repaint later!

Art, like nature, can serve as a great way to guide your taste and help you learn what works and what doesn't. Taking the Renoir painting of Romaine Lacaux depicted here: just focus on the colors and why they work. The dress takes center stage, and it is the colors that make it. If you'd translate this into a room design, I would take the white of the blouse as an anchor and frame, so the trim, the doors, and so on. The warm gray would go on the walls, but it would need to

BABE
RAINBOW

OPPOSITE The enfilade from the butler pantry toward the dining room at Puddleduck Farm shows how well the lacquered ceiling connects the different spaces. The green dining room is the focal point and draws the eye in. LEFT The unexpected red theory might be a TikTok buzzword but it always works. I've long loved combining pink with red and it helps frame the striking artwork by Ling Jian.

have the blue from the scalloped straps (maybe even with the scalloped design!) as well as the red from the flowers in her hand in a border or as a fake picture trim. Then you add a piece of furniture upholstered in a floral print, just like the one behind the young girl in the painting. Et voilà: you have created a totally unexpected color story, all based on one work of art.

Let me give you another, real life example: My most recent inspiration was a stained-glass window. It is in my mother-in-law's church just outside Antwerp, Belgium. The mass is in Flemish, so I don't understand a lot of it and my mind tends to wander. One summer, it wandered to one of the stained-glass windows, a rather modern one depicting the harvest, with the most vibrant Yves Klein blue for the sky and golden yellow wheat bushels. I already knew at that time that we would be moving to Connecticut, and that our future house would get new paint colors, at the very least. Little did I know that the bright blue and golden yellow palette would prove perfect for our north-facing kitchen. Having previously used a mustardy yellow in our sitting room in Shaker Heights, I knew the possible pitfalls of the color, namely

TOP The walls of the primary bedroom in Shaker Heights were driven by the colors of the curtains. We settled on Stiffkey Blue by Farrow & Ball after a good amount of testing. **RIGHT** The blue of the kitchen island is cleverly repeated in the butler pantry at Puddleduck Farm, creating a sense of cohesion between the spaces.

BABE

LEFT Nothing brought us more joy than the bright blue walls of the mudroom in Shaker Heights. The Yves Klein qualities of this shade of blue, Drawing Room Blue by Farrow & Ball, was my absolute pride, especially at night and looking in from the outside. It glowed. I cannot wait to use this color in another project. **TOP** Two spaces that confirm how well red works to lift a space and give it instant interest. The red chair from my old office is perfect for our son's blue and brown bedroom, while the wonderful art installation lifts the yellow of Hinrich and Wolfgang's house and gives it a contemporary note.

its infamous green tint in a sunny space. However, in the dark and moody kitchen, now brightened with additional windows, the yellow had the space to let the warm undertones come out. The bright blue added a pep that made the space surprising, and, you guessed, gave it just the right amount of tension.

Selecting the right wall color also involves lots of experimentation. Light, space orientation, and geography all influence how a color will appear. A south-facing room, for example, enhances warm tones, while a north-facing one can make cool hues feel stark. Testing samples in various spots and lighting conditions is essential to avoid surprises. I always paint a test around a window as well as door frames. It allows me to see the color against outside light and how it works transitioning into the next room.

I personally like to settle on one or two spaces in the house that will be the anchor for the whole scheme. This can also be something other than wall colors: Amanda's use of a lacquered ceiling throughout the first level of Puddleduck Farm creates a great connection between the older and newer parts of the house. In my Klosters home, I used red to create a common thread throughout the flat.

A special note about the house of Hinrich and Wolfgang in Hamburg: a citron yellow unifies the upper levels of the house, creating a sense of connection while allowing each room to maintain its distinct personality. The basement's warmer yellow complements its low ceilings and black-and-white flooring, showing how intentional adjustments can make bold choices work. I love this unique approach that makes the house even more special than it already is. The citron yellow is a bold choice but works well in the northern light of Hamburg. It can be found in many grand houses in the north to counteract the long and dark winters.

Choosing colors for your home can be daunting, but nothing is more rewarding than finding the right combination and bringing your vision to life. If you're not sure where to start, consider a favorite color and make a point of incorporating it into your scheme. (What is my favorite color you ask? I wouldn't be able to tell you because it changes daily!) And don't hesitate to be inspired by trends, though I suggest you try to look at them from a traditional perspective. Humanity has used wall colors since we've been living in houses. There is a good chance that a "new" trend is actually just reiterating a style that has been around for a long time. For example, unsure of using a bright green on the walls? Gregorian houses used green a lot as the paint had just been invented and was very trendy (as well as filled with arsenic, which, thankfully, isn't the case nowadays). It works beautifully and does not feel trendy at all—at least for the moment.

Still, colors for your home require you to be a little brave. By testing them out as much as you can, thinking of how they transition between rooms, and considering what you would like the overall scheme of the house to be, that bravery usually pays off. And if it doesn't? You can still make it work by tweaking other parts of your design. That's where the fun begins! ❖

Nothing is more fun than creating an interesting enfilade with colors. Done right, it will give your home the connection you want and leave a lasting impression. Hence my absolute tip for testing out wall colors: always test them around doorways as well so that you can gauge the effect of the color into the next space.

5-Minute Stories
CAT
DOG
MOO
Alphabet
DINOSNORES

Furniture Is More Than Practical

urniture is necessary, for obvious reasons. It is also the easiest way to imbue your home with the art of the clash or make it all look matchy-matchy. A mix of styles, periods, and finishes brings depth and vibrancy to interiors, creating that tension we are looking for. Whether it's a well-loved antique, a streamlined mid-century piece, or even IKEA, the furniture in your home can tell a story–ideally, several stories at once.

Classical furniture has stood the test of time for a reason. Pieces with clean lines, sturdy craftsmanship, and timeless appeal provide the perfect anchor for more daring design choices. A Chippendale chair, for instance, can hold its own in almost any interior, offering structure and sophistication while making room for other more playful elements.

Consider a traditional roll arm sofa: its deep and overstuffed seat and rolled arms exude comfort and grandeur, yet it pairs beautifully with a mid-century modern coffee table and a bold rug. The key to incorporating classical furniture is to let it ground the space, serving as a counterbalance to more eclectic or experimental pieces.

Well-made antiques can be the crown jewels of the art of the clash. Their craftsmanship and sense of history bring a depth that can be hard to replicate with newer furniture. A Biedermeier desk, for example, doesn't just serve a functional purpose–it becomes a conversation piece, a link to the past that enriches the present.

When incorporating antiques, think beyond their intended use. A chest of drawers can become a bathroom vanity, while a vintage dining table might work brilliantly as a desk. The beauty of antiques lies in their adaptability; they can bring a sense of tradition to a contemporary space or add texture and gravitas to a room filled with lighter, more modern elements.

Antique stores, thrift stores, flea markets, and online marketplaces are treasure troves for those willing to hunt for antiques and vintage pieces. The thrill of finding a unique piece is hard to beat and these items often add character and personality that mass-produced furniture lacks. Take the dining chairs in New Canaan: a *brocante*, or flea market, find that was exactly what the large and imposing dining room needs. I didn't feel any qualms painting and upholstering the postmodern chairs in the way I wanted. The key is to see the potential in pieces that others might overlook–something that's at the heart of the art of the clash.

Klosters
GRAUBÜNDEN · GRISONS

What would we do without chests of drawers? A favorite pastime of mine is an impatient DIY, and the blue-green tall commode (OPPOSITE) was just that. I found it online and spray-painted it in two hours. The bureau (TOP LEFT) was a present from my paternal grandmother. I particularly love the shape and color of it. And finally, the black lacquered and painted chest of drawers (TOP RIGHT) is actually a cleverly designed bureau that was another antique store find. I love its whimsical nature and its versatility.

A note on IKEA: Nowadays, IKEA offers more Scandi-minimalism, but it can still be the go-to for well-made basics. One of our sofas is an EKTORP that we purchased when we first got married. It has lived many lives and now sits happily in the library with a new yellow slipcover. I don't see the point of getting rid of it while it still works. One day, I will have the funds for the sofa of my dreams but until then, I'm very happy with our trusty IKEA piece.

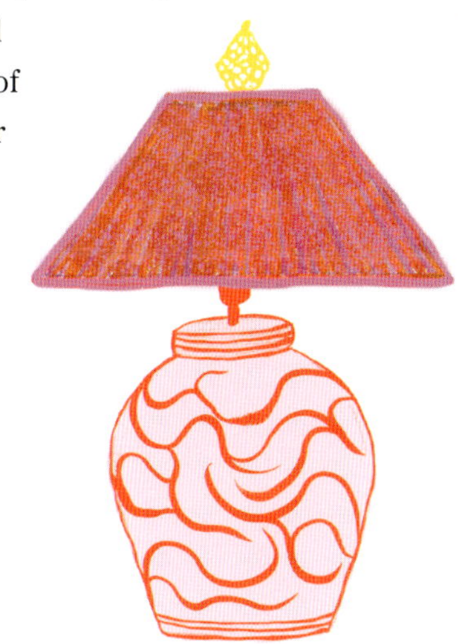

Mid-century modern (MCM) furniture is the bridge between classic English interiors and contemporary flair, making it a natural fit for the art of the clash. With clean lines, organic forms, and focus on functionality, mid-century pieces can temper the exuberance of bold colors and patterns, creating a balanced, cohesive look.

A sleek fifties lounge chair, for example, pairs surprisingly well with a traditional English

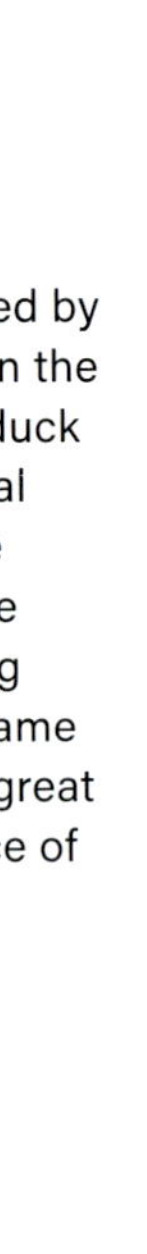

The desk (RIGHT) was designed by Amanda herself and stands in the green guest room at Puddleduck Farm. It shows that a practical piece can (and should!) have unusual style. The shelf in the primary bedroom in Hamburg (OPPOSITE) is painted in the same yellow as the walls, another great trick to make a practical piece of furniture work for you.

floral sofa. Similarly, a mid-century sideboard can provide a neutral base for a gallery wall filled with eclectic artwork. The beauty of mid-century modern lies in its simplicity—it enhances rather than competes, allowing other design elements to shine.

The key to mixing furniture styles is finding common threads. A shared color palette, complementary materials, or similar proportions can create harmony even when the pieces themselves are wildly different. For instance, a Louis XVI armchair reupholstered in a bold, modern fabric bridges the gap between eras, while a classic upholstered ottoman coffee table pairs effortlessly with a contemporary sectional.

Texture also plays a role. Pair a sleek lacquered table with an antique wooden bench or balance a plush velvet sofa with a minimalist metal side table. The contrast of textures adds depth and keeps the space from feeling one-dimensional.

Every piece of furniture in your home should feel like it belongs—not because it matches but because it contributes to the narrative. A thrifted chair might recall a memorable market trip, while a passed-down sideboard speaks to family history. By mixing pieces with personal significance alongside new finds, you create a home that feels authentic and alive. I can tell you a story about every single item in our home, and I feel connected to all of it.

Der Pakt
KOSMOS
Blue Note Photography
ROCK N' ROOTS
Woodstock
Lex Barker
CARY GRANT
CARY GRANT
CARY GRANT
CARY GRANT

STOP
RAINFOREST
DEFORESTATION
TESCO
NESCAFE
Palm Oil Free
Pedigree
SAVE
THE
FOREST
STOP
OUR PALM OIL
TOBLERONE
L'OREAL
THE BODY SHOP
Protect
Earth
P&G
Kraft
VOGUE
19

Gries.
69

LEFT The rattan coffee table by Sarah Ellison is one of the rare occasions where I bought something new. I fell in love with the shape and it has served us well, first in Shaker Heights and now in New Canaan. It adds a much-needed sense of contemporary to the spaces. **TOP** The round table that my parents bought it when I was six years old. It has seen laughter, tears, homework, long nights, long mornings, everything. I carved my name into the soft wood many times, and now my children do the same, which feels very special.

RIGHT A beautiful lacquered bamboo love seat upholstered in Cole & Son in the kitchen at Puddleduck Farm. **OPPOSITE** A Biedermeier armoire from a brocante in Switzerland hides the TV behind a clever *trompe l'oeuil* door. The armchair in front is from my grandparents in a typical MCM style that gets cozier with the inexpensive reindeer fur to make it feel more Alpine for the flat in Klosters.

In practice, the art of the clash might look like this: a classical roll-arm sofa paired with a mid-century modern side table, an antique mirror above a sleek console, and a thrifted armchair reupholstered in a new print. The interplay of styles, materials, and finishes creates a space that feels layered and dynamic, a true reflection of its inhabitants.

Furniture is more than just functional; it's the framework that defines your home. By embracing a mix of styles—classic, antique, mid-century, and thrifted—you can create interiors that are rich in character and endlessly fascinating. The beauty of the art of the clash lies in its inclusivity, its ability to combine the old and the new, the ornate and the simple, into something uniquely personal. After all, the most memorable spaces are the ones that tell a story—and what better way to tell yours than through the furniture you choose? ❖

THE GREAT
PALMIST

TOP A handpainted sideboard in the typical Alpine style sits next to a contemporary piece of photography in the flat in Klosters. OPPOSITE TOP The mix of contemporary, MCM, and antique pieces of furniture make the living room feel light, airy, and of this time. OPPOSITE BOTTOM LEFT The bamboo nightstand comes from Hong Kong and adds to the tropical mood in this bedroom at Puddleduck Farm. OPPOSITE BOTTOM RIGHT The blue spindle bed adds the pop of color needed in this children's bedroom in Shaker Heights.

Not a single piece of furniture on these two pages was purchased new, except for the black Chinese lacquer shelf in the OPPOSITE TOP LEFT photo, which was made to order in Singapore to hold our TV (duly put away for the sake of the shot). Everything else was either inherited (the trunk in the OPPOSITE TOP RIGHT and the chest of drawers ABOVE) or reused, like the cabinet in the OPPOSITE BOTTOM RIGHT that had been part of the original butler pantry in Shaker Heights. And the BOTTOM LEFT is the pine closet built in the guest bathroom in Shaker Heights, still in pristine condition at the ripe old age of 100 years.

THE ANATOMY OF COLOUR
THE STORY OF ART
KATY HESSEL
LALLA ESSAYDI
SURF STYLE AT HOME
DÉCORS BARBARES
A TALE OF INTERIORS
PIERCE & WARD
DICTIONARY

Interlude

FREEDOM
UNRULY
Caste

A Tale of Two Houses: Shaker Heights and New Canaan

Hindsight is a powerful tool in life and in interior design. It teaches us to reflect on past choices, informs future decisions, and evolves our personal style. The renovation of our 1920 Tudor house in Shaker Heights was my first true foray into interior design, while our current home in New Canaan stands as a testament to how far I've come as a designer.

The Shaker Heights house marked my introduction to large-scale renovations. While we had remodeled lightly in Luxembourg, this was the first time I was involved every step of the way. It felt grown-up, daunting, and exhilarating. Living in Singapore at the time, I knew I needed support to manage such a significant project from afar, so I enlisted the help of Dawn Cook and her team. Dawn became not only my guide through the process but also a dear friend and an inspiration who convinced me to pursue interior design professionally.

Like many older homes, the Shaker Heights house required far more work than we'd anticipated. What began as a plan to update the kitchen and add a mudroom quickly expanded to include rewiring the electrical system, upgrading the HVAC, and taking down the exhaust chimney brick-by-brick to accommodate the new kitchen layout.

To complicate matters, we purchased the house in January 2020 and began renovations just as the world shut down. My February visit to Shaker Heights would be my last trip before lockdowns took effect, leaving Dawn to manage the project in my absence. By the time we arrived in August, the house was far from complete. Strangely, this worked to my advantage—it gave me hands-on experience and a deeper understanding of the craft, even amid the chaos of an unfinished home.

Compared to Shaker Heights, renovating our home in New Canaan was a breeze. We purchased the house via video call—an expat necessity in a tight housing market—and decided to live in it for a while before making major changes. This approach was a direct lesson from Shaker Heights: it's essential to get a feel for a space before deciding what to change, and it wasn't long before the kitchen (again!) became my focus. The dated style wasn't my favorite, but the main issue was that the layout was entirely wrong for our family.

TOP The primary bedroom in Shaker Heights got its dark blue walls from the blue in the curtains. The rattan headboard came from Singapore; the wall hanging I inherited from my mother. It is a wraparound shawl, and incidentally one of my most beloved possessions. LEFT The rattan headboard was of course reused, but looks very different in the primary bedroom in New Canaan. By painting the ceiling in the same warm beige, Roman Plaster by Little Greene Paint, the feeling of this space is softer and feels like a warm hug. I also reused the curtains from Shaker Heights in this room and their effect is again a completely different one.

The kitchen in Shaker Heights, which Dawn designed with a great eye for detail. The arched backsplash was created out of necessity as the marble cracked when it was installed, originally being of full height. This proved to be the necessary cherry on top for this fabulous kitchen, and inspired a few friends in their kitchen designs, which we always felt was the greatest compliment. Including the original butler pantry in the kitchen required careful calibration and a good amount of skill but we were so happy it worked out.

The kitchens in Shaker Heights and New Canaan represent two distinct points in my design journey. In Shaker Heights, preserving the original butler's pantry cabinets was a priority. Dawn designed a scheme that beautifully incorporated its cabinetry alongside new elements: a central island, fresh cabinets, and a breakfast nook. While the kitchen was functional and elegant, I realized over time that it didn't feel entirely like me.

This time, I tackled the design alone, without Dawn's guidance, and I approached it with a newfound confidence born from my experiences in Shaker Heights. One of the biggest lessons I'd learned was my dislike of kitchen islands. Once a dream symbol of an "American" kitchen, I found them bulky, unmovable, and dominating. This informed the New Canaan kitchen, which had a dated layout that didn't work for our family. A large island was centered in the space, and the lack of natural light made the room feel cramped.

I decided to forego an island entirely, instead focusing on creating an airy, light-filled space by removing upper cabinets and replacing them with windows flanking the oven range. The result is a colorful, inviting room that balances functionality with personality.

Shaker Heights was also where I rediscovered my love of color, though not without missteps. Inspired by my mother's fondness for yellows in the nineties, I chose golden yellow for the living room walls. Initially, I was convinced Sudbury Yellow by Farrow & Ball was perfect but seeing it in the space revealed it was too bright. After testing other shades, we settled on the richer India Yellow. While I loved the warmth this brought, the project revealed my inexperience in creating a cohesive scheme. Budget constraints meant many walls remained white, unintentionally serving as a palate cleanser between the colorful spaces.

Our kitchen in New Canaan feels completely different to the Shaker Heights one. I went for saturated colors, and I love how it turned out and helps the kitchen glow, even with its north-facing gloominess. The unusual backsplash design was inspired by how the original marble slab had cracked on one corner. Another example of how all of these renovations and remodels are only possible with some truly amazing artisans on your side: the design was carved by hand and looks exactly like the broken-off piece I was inspired by.

In New Canaan, I approached color with greater intention. Two spaces—the yellow and blue kitchen and the rose-pink living room—anchored the palette for the entire house. The library with its jewel-green walls complemented both, while the hallways tied everything together: the front entry painted in cognac brown and the back hallway in a soft grayish blue-green. The result is a home that feels unified yet vibrant, bold yet balanced.

The Shaker Heights experience taught me practical lessons—how to manage renovations, respect a home's history, and navigate design decisions—but it also shaped my confidence. Dawn's modern-traditional aesthetic complemented my eclectic style, and she encouraged me to take the lead in choosing colors and finishes. This collaboration laid the foundation for my evolution as a designer.

By the time we moved to New Canaan, I felt ready to tackle the house on my own. Living in the space before making changes allowed me to understand its quirks and potential, ensuring the design reflected both our family's needs and my growing sense of self-assurance.

If Shaker Heights was my initiation into design, a blend of trial, error, and discovery, New Canaan represented a more confident chapter. The former taught me the value of collaboration and the importance of hindsight, while the latter allowed me to trust my instincts and embrace creative risks.

These two houses may be separated by miles and years, but they share a common thread: the lessons they taught me about design, growth, and myself. They are not just houses but milestones in a journey that continues to evolve—a testament to the power of reflection, creativity, and the joy of making a house a home. ❖

PATTERNS
THE ANATOMY OF COLOUR
THE STORY OF ART
KATY HESSEL
LALLA ESSAYDI
GEORGIA O'KEEFFE
SURF STYLE AT HOME
DÉCORS BARBARES
A TALE OF INTERIORS

SHORT CUTS
LALLA ESSAYDI

All About Art (And I Don't Mean Family Photos)

You may have noticed that wall art plays a big role in all the interiors showcased in this book. I'm sometimes surprised when some gloriously decorated homes fall short because the art on the walls feels meaningless or too generic. For a room to sing, art should play a prominent role. It anchors spaces, draws the eye, and provides a counterpoint to other design elements. Without art, a room can feel incomplete, no matter how well-designed. By integrating it thoughtfully and creatively, you can transform your space into a true reflection of your individuality. After all, a house that becomes a home is one that tells a story—and what better way to tell your story than through the art you choose to surround yourself with?

More than just an accessory, art is the soul of a home and nowhere is this truer than in the art of the clash. In every space, art acts as the finishing layer, the dynamic element that transforms a beautifully designed room into something extraordinary. It provides personality, intrigue, and, most importantly, contrast—the tension that lies at the heart of this design philosophy. Art isn't just decoration; it's storytelling, a way to reflect who you are and what you love.

Art has the magical power of transforming a space in an instant. The entry hall in New Canaan could veer too saccharine and old school if not for the contemporary art in strict black and white. Similarly, at Puddleduck Farm, the green lacquered walls of the dining room are stunning on their own, but the addition of bold, layered art transforms the space into something extraordinary where the eye wants to travel from piece to piece.

A side note on family photos: I understand the urge to print them out and display them prominently. However, a gallery wall solely consisting of family photos doesn't exactly scream art of the clash. Personally, I prefer to have family photos in standing frames on dressers or sideboards. A true and tested approach is displaying them in a powder room, counteracting the ostentatiousness personal photos can bring with them.

But if you would like a gallery wall with family photos, try mixing it up with other personal artifacts, such as kids' drawings or other memorabilia that can add different textures and shapes, and place it somewhere you can enjoy it, such as a TV room or hallway that is frequently used.

FRANK ZAPPA
PORTUGAL
Freuet euch im Herrn
HERBERT LIST
MÖBEL
Frauen in der Architektur
GUSTAV KLIMT
Karl Schmidt-Rottluff
DOMESTIC ART

Two great examples of using everyday objects as art. These pieces clearly carry meaning for Hinrich and Wolfgang, and they add to the story and charm of their expansive town house in Hamburg.

Building an art collection may sound intimidating, but it needn't be. The best collections begin with a single piece that resonates with you. Visit local galleries, artist markets, or even online platforms to explore works that speak to your personal taste. Emerging artists offer incredible value, and their pieces often come with a story that makes them even more special. A single, well-chosen piece can elevate an entire room, becoming the focal point around which the rest of the design revolves.

Art doesn't have to come in a frame. Many objects, when displayed with intention, can become art. For instance, in the TV room of Wolfgang and Hinrich's Hamburg home, a mix of band T-shirts, festival lanyards, and even traffic cones adorn the walls. It creates a space that is visually interesting and deeply personal. It reflects the lives of its owners in a way no generic print ever could.

Textiles, too, are art. A classic tapestry or colorful *suzani*—those beautiful works of tapestry that traditionally were parts of a dowry in many Islamic countries—can create an oversized statement piece that anchors a room wonderfully. A vintage scarf, maybe framed or just nailed into the wall, can add softness and texture to a space.

While walls are the obvious place for art, consider more unconventional placements to fully embrace the art of the clash. Lean framed pieces on a mantel or console table offer a relaxed, curated look. Use narrow shelves to layer pieces of varying heights and textures.

TOP LEFT The space above a table, be it big or small, is the ideal spot for large-scale installations or artworks. In the guest room in Klosters I used a series of decoupage art to fill the white wall. In the hallway at Puddleduck Farm, TOP RIGHT, Amanda used the awkward focal point between the two doorways as a moment for the beautiful photograph. And in the living room in New Canaan, OPPOSITE, the large-scale oil painting serves to balance out the more saccharine tones of the wall, while also adhering to the overall theme of the human form that prevails in the space.

Art has the unique ability to change the mood and meaning of a room—and the key comes back to contrast. A traditional room with classic furniture benefits from a modern, abstract piece that adds tension and intrigue. Conversely, a highly contemporary space can be softened and given depth with vintage or representational works. The tension between the two creates the magic. In my own experience, a contemporary black-and-white piece kept an otherwise traditional entryway from feeling overly quaint, while a mix of bold and unique works made the white walls in Klosters interesting to look at.

Curating art for your home isn't about matching; it's about layering and creating relationships between pieces. When designing a space, I usually have one or two pieces of art in mind that determine the style or feel of all the art in the space. For example, in our bedroom in New Canaan we hung only abstract art. Choosing a style before I started to style the room in earnest made the choices easier. Another trick I used was to stick to a certain color palette.

F&M

JB

TOP My mother's living room in the flat where I grew up in Hamburg. The whole place was full of contemporary art, which she collected with a small budget but with great joy. **RIGHT** The artwork above the orange chest of drawers picks up the accent colors in the primary bedroom in New Canaan, and sticks to the theme for the room, which only has abstract artworks.

The dominating colors in the room are the light brown (one might say "beige," but we try to avoid that word, ha!) and orange and red tones. The art reflects the colors and expands on them, adding some pinks and golds to the mix.

Every room benefits from art, from the kitchen to the living room, but the seriousness can vary depending on the space. A small connecting hallway in Shaker Heights didn't feel like it warranted much decor, but it was a high traffic space. I didn't want to hang anything too serious or too high value, so I used posters in oversized frames with red mats. The inexpensive solution added a colorful layer while not stressing me out if my kids touched or bumped into them.

At its core, the art of the clash is about creating spaces that resonate on a deeply personal level, and art is one of the most effective tools for achieving this. Whether you're starting with a single print or curating a multi-piece collection, let your choices reflect your personality, your story, and your willingness to embrace the unexpected. ❖

LEFT The living room of Hinrich and Wolfgang in Hamburg. The beaded side table is a work of art in itself, while the oversized paper work adds some calm to the mix of colors. TOP I love using large posters to give a space some interest, especially on white walls. The balustrade hallway in Shaker Heights looked lovely with them.

BROMLEY

TOP A small abstract collage work above the headboard in the primary bedroom in New Canaan. The arched headboard doesn't lend itself to a big piece of art so this was a good solution. BOTTOM RIGHT Nothing beats a mix of family photos and art in a powder room. The little shelf is perfect to display this mix, hung on the wall behind the toilet in the New Canaan guest loo. OPPOSITE All the browns in the hall in New Canaan needed a good counter, and the oversized photo work by Giovanni Castell does just the trick. It is also a truly large piece of art that needs its space, so this is a perfect spot for it.

Another round of anything can serve as art. Or at least as decorative art. I also like to be creative with the framing of pieces (LEFT). The stuffed pheasant is a statement that I loved for that location, leaning a bit more into the traditional look of the hallway in Shaker Heights (TOP).

John Lennon
SAINT X ALEXIS SCHAITKIN
T.C. BOYLE · OUTSIDE LOOKING IN

Nudge
DARE MORE BOLDLY
MICHAEL LEWIS FLASH BOYS
SPEECHES THAT CHANGED THE WORLD

How Lighting Can Cozy Up a Space

Lighting is an essential part in any home. Much has been said about layering lights, but I really want to reiterate how important it is to create various levels of light and luminosity. Like with bland art, I've seen many spaces that are exquisitely decorated but seem to be missing all kinds of cozy lighting.

Just as contrasting styles and materials create visual excitement, layered and varied lighting creates depth, mood, and functionality in a space. The secret lies in embracing a mix of lights and thinking creatively about how each contributes to the overall feel of the space.

If there is anything that I want you to take away from this chapter, it is to abandon the single ceiling light. Nothing makes a space colder and less inviting than a single light source from above. The direction of the light creates harsh shadows, counteracting any attempt at coziness and intimacy. You also want to have light coming from various sources, not just one. Again, all for the sake of creating an atmosphere you want to spend time and stay in. If you must have a ceiling light for practical purposes, be sure to make it a warm light, be it through mini lampshades, a warm light bulb, or recessed lights that are placed at various spots on the ceiling.

Now that I've gotten that off my chest, let's look at the various ways of lighting a space. Just as design relies on layers—paint, furniture, textiles—lighting too should be layered. The three main types of lighting—ceiling, task, and table—serve different purposes but come together to create a pleasant atmosphere.

- Ceiling or Ambient Lighting is the foundational layer, the general illumination that ensures a room feels bright enough to move through comfortably. This can be ceiling lights, recessed lighting, chandeliers, or even wall sconces. Large floor lamps are also a great way to raise light and spread it far.

- Task Lighting is functional, focusing light where it's needed most. Desk lamps, reading lights, and under-cabinet kitchen lighting fall into this category. These add purpose to the space while also contributing to the overall design. Personally, I love a good but pretty task light in the kitchen. I turn off any overhead lights and let the other lights shine; they provide a more indirect light source and make a kitchen dinner all the more cozy.

- Table Lamps are what we use the most as they illuminate enough, but not too much, and help set the tone of a space. Play with the height of the table lamp as well as with the height of the furniture you place it on. Table lamps are also the best way to add color and texture. Pair a colorful base with a pleated fabric lampshade and it becomes an immediate eye catcher.

Lamps are an expensive part of renovation, which makes it an area where I rely heavily on antique and thrift stores as well as online marketplaces. There are also a few budget friendly ways to create your own table lamps. For example, I DIY'd a pair of oversized, decorative wine bottles into table lamps with the help of some Home Depot trips and YouTube.

You can also consider more traditional lighting: candles! Don't underestimate how much light candles can bring. My mother used a chandelier with real candles in one iteration of her dining room, and I was always surprised by how bright they were. I did the same with candle sconces in our home in Shaker Heights. While they might not be practical for day-to-day lighting, they are a great add-on for the sake of coziness.

Good lighting isn't just about brightness; it's about creating depth. The interplay of light and shadow gives a room its character, much like the tension between design elements that defines the art of the

LONDON
ABE
INBOW
2022
PINOT NOIR
Jordan

OPPOSITE The under-cabinet light in the butler pantry at Puddleduck Farm. It's not just practical but also lends a festive mood to the space; very fitting as it's often used during dinner parties. **LEFT** Nothing is more simple than a nightstand with a lamp. The fabric-pleated lampshade makes this a very cozy iteration, perfect for the pink and yellow guest room in Shaker Heights.

clash. Highlighting contrasts—soft glows against darker corners, spotlights on textured surfaces—creates a layered, dynamic effect. For instance, an ornate chandelier in an entryway might cast dramatic shadows on the walls, adding dimension to the space. In a kitchen, soft under-cabinet lighting combined with a bold, sculptural pendant can make even a small space feel luxurious.

My main tip for everyone updating their lighting is to install dimmer switches wherever possible. The ability to control brightness transforms a room's mood from functional to mellow to dramatic with the flick of a switch. In a dining room, dimmed overhead lights paired with candlelight and lamps strategically placed in corners create intimacy, while in a living room, softly glowing table lamps make the space feel inviting after sunset. Chandeliers especially can be too bright, so making them dimmable means you are more likely to use them.

Lighting isn't just functional; it's an integral part of the design process. By layering different types of light, mixing styles, and embracing the interplay of brightness and shadow, you can create a home that feels alive, welcoming, and uniquely yours. With a thoughtful approach to lighting, every room can shine—literally and figuratively—transforming your house into a harmonious blend of contrasts that sing together in perfect clashing harmony. ❖

casterman
Zeichenschule

Powder rooms are always a favorite way to be whimsical and lighting can create some great contrasts to make them even more interesting. The blue glass pendant added a much-needed clash in the high-gloss red powder room in Shaker Heights (LEFT). The very small powder room in the basement in New Canaan comes with a brass plate light next to the sink and a sconce that is offset behind the toilet. This actually creates a soft light which is so preferable in a powder room (TOP).

PLATO
KLEIST
RYOKAN
HARUKI MURAKAMI

WÖLFE
DAS AMT
H.G. WELLS
DIE MANNS
Christopher Clark
VILLEN IN VENETIEN
DER LETZTE ZAR
PORTUGAL

TOP A little table lamp in the corner of the very functional kitchen in the flat in Klosters. I love using the rechargeable lamps which are now widely available to add another source of cozy light to a space. **RIGHT** Table lamps come in all shapes and forms. The Stiffel brass lamp with its woven lampshade was yet another brocante find and is just the right size, as it's high enough not to shine in your eyes when standing at the bar cart.

THE

Anything Can Be Something Else (Or, Creative Ways to Rethink Materials)

"Anything can be a curtain if you want it to be," I told my husband as I hung yet another tablecloth as a drapery panel in Klosters. That statement captures my entire philosophy of home design: thinking outside the box can unlock limitless possibilities. Reimagining an object's purpose can elevate a space, solve design dilemmas, and bring a sense of playfulness and individuality to your home.

Table linens as curtains might seem obvious, but they're a favorite of mine for a reason. The textures, patterns, and sizes of tablecloths often lend themselves beautifully to drapery. Similarly, curtains don't always need to divide the inside from the outside. Consider using them instead of doors on a pantry or under a sink. I changed the use of the original pantry in New Canaan, which was a hallway pantry with doors, and use it for all our extra china and kitchen machines now. I desperately hated the doors on that thing, they were horribly in the way. We took them off and added a curtain rod and some very simple curtains we had left over. Not only is it one million times more practical to access, but the curtains also added another textured layer to the hallway, which feels pretty and intentional.

Now, drapery and textiles can be expensive. In particular, when you have to create window treatments for a whole house, the prices can quickly soar into five digits. Using good quality secondhand drapery from thrift stores can help with the budget as well as make spaces more unique. Using a tablecloth as a decorative curtain can work well to cut down on cost. You need to use clips and curtain rings to hang them, and they will never feel as heavily luxurious as a drapery shawl. Still, I love using them for spaces that don't need a customized window treatment or a blackout treatment, like in the basement living room in our home in New Canaan.

Next up, furniture designed for one purpose often works beautifully for another. Vintage trunks, for example, make excellent coffee tables that can double as stylish storage solutions. Their solid construction and weathered patina add character to a living room, while their hidden storage makes them practical in smaller spaces.

501
REBEL YELL
Romance of the Three Kingdoms
Why You Say It
Henry Kissinger
On China
AUREL STEIN
JOHN HOWARD
HONG KONG EYE
THE CAPTAIN CLASS
1776
LIEBLING
THE PARTNERSHIP
MEXICO
THE COOKBOOK
LOVE LEMONS
MINISTRY OF FOOD
MODERN VIEWS
WINE ATLAS
Yves Saint Laurent
AMERICA
THE COOKBOOK

BHUTAN
INDIA
NEPAL
BURMA
Mongolia
New Zealand
Tibet
Cambodia
Australia
China
China
Japan
Nepal
THAILAND
India
India

My parents were very creative in creating furniture in their first apartment in Paris in the seventies: my mother dreamed of round side tables, but they were out of their budget. My father came up with an ingenious solution by using heavy garbage bins, on top of which he screwed round sheets of plywood. My mother threw a tablecloth over each—another textile layer—and the round side tables I grew up with were born.

Beyond tablecloths, other textiles can be used in unexpected places. A beautifully patterned kilim rug makes for a stunning headboard or wall hanging, instantly adding another layer to a room. Similarly, a quilt or a vintage suzani can be used over a sofa or an armchair as a slipcover to change the look.

Sometimes it isn't the objects you're adding that might be thought about unconventionally, it's the spaces themselves. I've seen plenty of homes with spaces that seem ill-suited for their intended purpose—awkward hallways, oddly shaped alcoves or former sleeping porches like the one in our Shaker Heights home. It was tagged onto the former primary bedroom for the house, which we knew quickly we would use as a children's bedroom. A "sleeping porch" is so called because it was used for sleeping during the hot summer months, with all windows open. It is always at the farthest part of a house and only has one wall, with the other four walls made up of windows. Ours even had the disadvantage of coming with two doors.

None of this screamed bedroom, but we made it work by leaving one of the doors closed and covering it with a tablecloth. Our daughter's bed stood in front of the door on one side, while her brother's bed was placed on the other side of the door, also covered with a wall hanging to make it cozier.

That was already enough to make the small room feel larger. Paired with kantha cloth (wonderfully colorful bed throws) as window treatments, their room became a warm and inviting space.

Incidentally, we had used the same fabric as a decorative curtain in our second home as a young family, all the way back in Luxembourg. Our daughter was young when we lived in Shaker Heights and she absolutely loved her bedroom—so much so that she spent hours playing in it. Anyone with small children knows what I mean when I say that this was the biggest compliment. Thinking outside the box often reveals creative solutions.

This approach isn't just about utility; it's also about embracing the unexpected. Repurposing materials adds an element of whimsy and personal touch to a space. One of my favorite pieces in Klosters is a vintage armoire, beautifully painted in the folklore style of the region. Our kitchen is unfortunately just too small to be an eat-in kitchen for all five of us, so I decided to forgo a table and chairs and just use the armoire as extra storage. It adds a beautiful layer to the space and has informed the decoration of the whole room.

If you're new to reimagining materials, start with a question: *What do I need, and what do I already have that might fulfill that need?* This mindset has guided countless design decisions in my own life. When we couldn't find the perfect bedside tables for a rental, we repurposed wooden crates. I'm currently writing this sitting at my desk, which is the dining table we used in Shaker Heights but have now pushed against the windows in my studio/dining room so I can look outside.

Departure
Luc Tuymans
BASQUIAT
TASCHEN
MARX
MARX
FELIX VALLOTTON
HENRI MATISSE
Manet
Vilhelm Hammershøi

LEFT Antique leather luggage serves as a place to add some more books but also as a way to store items that we don't need every day in the flat in Klosters. **TOP** The kilim thrown over the sofa helps to balance the yellow of it, and the tapestry on the wall is a great focal point in the primary bedroom of Hinrich and Wolfgang in Hamburg. The tiger is obviously the main character.

At the heart of this philosophy is, again, the simple mantra of *say yes*. Say yes to the table linens that might make perfect curtains, to the vintage trunk that could double as a coffee table, to the armoire that you might not have an immediate spot for. By opening yourself to possibilities, you create a home that is not only functional but deeply personal.

Creativity flourishes when you embrace the potential in everyday objects. A vintage tin can be reworked to become a lamp. Anything can be art; just check out the traffic cones hung on the wall in Hinrich and Wolfgang's TV room. A bookshelf can serve as much prettier storage in a mudroom than any cubby stack. When you start thinking beyond conventional uses, you'll discover that anything can be something else—and that's where the magic happens. ❖

HERGÉ
INÉDITE
TINTIN
EN
AMÉRIQUE

TOP A woven cloth from Laos hangs in the children's bedroom in Klosters. The white walls need a lot of color to offset the stark white. **RIGHT** The sleep sofa is hidden under an old kantha cloth, while the wardrobe is covered by a block-print tablecloth that we hung up with tracks on the ceiling.

OPPOSITE Yet another use of a textile to hide something. However, in this case, the hallway in New Canaan was tight because of the pantry doors. The curtains that replaced them not only look gorgeous but are also way more practical. LEFT Three pieces of furniture that didn't get a new upholstery but rather a throw or a slipcover to change their look. This is the most practical solution with children, in my book, as everything can be washed. BOTTOM The lacquer trays are practical in the butler pantry at Puddleduck Farm but mainly serve as a gorgeous backsplash, adding another layer of interest. NEXT PAGE The Chinese lacquer and gold screen is used as a wall hanging in the living room of Hinrich and Wolfgang in Hamburg, while the wooden pillars make it stand out even more.

PART TWO

We often talk about individual rooms—kitchens, bedrooms, living rooms, dining rooms—as if they exist entirely on their own, each with its own identity and purpose. But it's the relationships between these spaces that shape the experience of a home. How they connect, how they transition, how they differ and relate—all of this informs how a house feels. It's why I believe in the idea of spaces rather than simply rooms.

Spaces, to me, are defined environments within the home. They serve different needs and should have different moods. The kitchen, for example, is often the engine of the house—a place of activity, food, and, ideally, conversation. A bedroom is a refuge, somewhere to retreat and unwind. The dining room is a gathering space, sometimes formal, sometimes relaxed, but always a stage for connection. The living room might be the heart, a place for lingering, reading, watching, talking. And then there are the others: libraries, hallways, mudrooms, offices—each playing a supporting role in the rhythm of the home.

What I find difficult with the increasingly popular open-plan concept is that it flattens all of these distinctions. While it offers light and flow and the seductive idea of togetherness, I find that open-plan spaces can be loud, undefined, and emotionally flat. Without walls, everything is always happening all at once. There's nowhere for the eye—or the mind—to rest.

I often hear people talk about knocking down walls "to open things up," and while I understand the appeal in theory, I also think we've gone too far. A well-placed wall, a door you can close, or even just a strong sense of zoning, gives a space its own personality. It allows it to serve a clear purpose. Most importantly, it gives you a sense of belonging and safety.

That said, I do believe that all these spaces should speak to one another. A home works best when its rooms are in conversation, when you can feel the same hand behind each one, even if the mood shifts. This doesn't mean everything needs to match, but rather that there is a notion of a thread of style that weaves itself throughout the home. Every project in this book has this thread, and you notice it immediately when you set foot in them.

Ultimately, defining your spaces doesn't mean being rigid. It means giving each part of your home the opportunity to become what it wants to be. A reading nook that's quiet and tucked away. A dining room that sparkles with life. A bedroom that feels enveloping. A mudroom that is practical but pretty enough that you might just want to be tidy.

By resisting the urge to make everything open and everything visible, you give your home a sense of rhythm. Rooms become destinations. Activities have their rightful place. And the overall effect is one of balance: a house that is dynamic, layered, and, above all, lived in.

The Kitchen. Ah, the Kitchen . . .

Kitchens hold a central place in our lives, often becoming more than just a space to cook—they are places to gather, eat, and connect. As such, they have taken on outsized importance in the design world, often standing as the (very expensive) crown jewel of a home. While the emphasis on kitchen design can be debated, the reality is that we all eat every day and therefore spend a lot of time there. This makes it all the more essential to create a space that feels both functional and deeply personal.

Bringing the art of the clash into a kitchen might feel daunting. After all, kitchens are highly practical spaces and transforming them often requires more time, effort, and budget than other rooms. However, even in the blandest white rental kitchen, there are countless ways to introduce vibrancy, personality, and the tension that we crave.

Cabinetry is often the most visible element in a kitchen, and its style and finish set the tone for the entire space. A memorable example comes from a friend's mother, whose kitchen features light wooden cabinets paired with a deep blue backsplash. The craftsmanship of the cabinetry carries the room, and the bold blue accent reflects her distinctive taste. This is a kitchen that could only belong to her—a perfect embodiment of combining style and function.

Similarly, colorful cabinetry can make a striking statement. In our Shaker Heights kitchen, we opted for green cabinets complemented by pink walls. The combination added vibrancy and energy to the space, proving that a bold palette can work wonders in a kitchen. The key is to think beyond one isolated splash of color. A navy blue cabinet paired with all-white walls feels unfinished; instead, you could consider painting cabinetry, walls, and even floors in the same tones to create a striking monochrome look.

Color transforms kitchens into more than just functional spaces. Amanda's kitchen at Puddleduck Farm demonstrates this beautifully. The white cabinetry is offset by a dark gray-blue island, while a gray marble tulip table anchors the space. Above the table hangs a modern rustic light, and the addition of a Chinese lacquer bench and contemporary artwork brings in unexpected layers. The butler's pantry, painted the same dark blue as the island, creates a sense of flow leading to the green lacquered dining room.

OPPOSITE The tulip table at Puddleduck Farm serves as the center of family life. The modern shape, paired with the 1970s chairs, shows Amanda's incredible skill at lifting the 250-year-old farmhouse into contemporary times. **LEFT** The pantry at Puddleduck Farm is low, tiled, and full of a wonderful collection of crockery. Just what one imagines at a farmhouse.

In Hamburg, Wolfgang and Hinrich chose pale apple-green cabinetry that complements the citron yellow scheme running through their home. Their small kitchen, centered around an original butcher block, is a testament to their love of cooking and hosting. The combination of bold colors and vintage craftsmanship makes the space both personal and practical.

Art is as important in kitchens as it is in any other room. It elevates the space, adds character, and tells a story. I love using food-themed artwork or pieces that feel intrinsically tied to the kitchen—playful and perhaps a bit thematic, but never gimmicky. Plates, whether hung on walls or displayed on open shelves, are another way to incorporate art. Mixing crockery from different eras enhances the layered tension that makes a kitchen come alive.

Furthermore, the kitchen invites itself to more eclectic artwork. Vintage advertising, menus that mean something to you, children's art, or your favorite recipe can all be framed and hung, adding to the personality of the space. These touches make the kitchen feel connected to its purpose while adding an element of surprise.

Incorporating real furniture beyond cabinetry into a kitchen adds a unique and comfy layer. If space allows, include a real dining table with chairs or a bench rather than relying solely on bar seating. While bar seating is popular, particularly in American kitchens, I find they

The arched backsplash in the Shaker Heights kitchen was born out of necessity but became one of the most striking features of the kitchen.

often fall short in creating space for genuine conversation to occur. A table, on the other hand, invites gathering and adaptability–it can be replaced, moved, or resized as needed.

Amanda's tulip table at Puddleduck Farm is a perfect example. It is the center of her home, serving as a dining table, her workstation, and the place her family gathers. Its style contributes to the room's layered aesthetic. Similarly, a vintage farmhouse table or a sleek mid-century modern design can bring character to the space, offering contrast to traditional cabinetry or modern finishes.

Lighting in a kitchen plays a vital role, but don't fall into the trap of making it uniformly bright for every occasion and task. While task lighting is essential for functionality, overly bright, uniform lighting can strip a kitchen of its charm. Instead, embrace a mix of light sources to create ambiance and intimacy.

For example, in our Shaker Heights kitchen, we installed oversized pendants with round, floppy brass shades above the island. Their scale and shape created a contrast with the traditional cabinetry and green palette, introducing a touch of whimsy and drama. Adding a table lamp to a kitchen counter is another favorite trick of mine–it softens the space and makes it feel more inviting, especially during evening meals.

OTTOLENGHI
Nigel Slater

The New Canaan kitchen in all its glory. We added the two windows around the range, moved the fridge to the other side of the room, and painted the wooden floors, among many other things.

Stone countertops are an effective, yet pricey, way to add to your art of the clash. Which type of stone you choose is entirely down to your preferences and budget, but it can elevate a kitchen to another level. A unique backsplash design is another way to imbue your style. Both Shaker Heights and New Canaan boast unusual backsplash designs. Both have marble countertops and backsplashes, a material I love for its versatility and warmth, especially in the honed (instead of polished) styles I prefer.

Obviously, countertops can be made of many other materials than stone. You can get very colorful with Formica, which I love. Tiling is also making a comeback. As usual, it's down to preference and budget. The main takeaway here is to give it a good and long think: what do you need and want from your countertops? For example, I love to bake, and marble is simply the best to hand knead dough. It's a small thing, but it makes me extremely happy to be able

How I imagined the very cozy breakfast nook in the Shaker Heights kitchen, and how it actually turned out. It shows how structural things can be planned ahead but that the actual decorating of a space often changes in the moment.

to use our counters for exactly that purpose. Window treatments and soft furnishings, such as pillows on seating, add a comfortable layer to your kitchen. It's another layer of color and pattern that you can play with.

Finally, consider the smaller details that give a kitchen its unique personality. Hardware, for example, can completely transform the look of cabinetry. Opt for vintage brass pulls or colorful ceramic knobs to add texture. Functional items can also double as decor. A row of mismatched wooden cutting boards leaning against a backsplash, a vintage pitcher used as a utensil holder, or an open shelf lined with spice jars in mismatched containers all add depth and interest. These details might seem small, but they are the building blocks of a kitchen that feels layered, personal, and alive.

Balancing color, art, furniture, and lighting creates a kitchen that transforms this hard-working room into the heart of your home. Whether you're working with a blank canvas or enhancing an existing space, remember that the best kitchens tell a story—your story. Let it be vibrant, layered, and wholly yours. ❖

♨酒温泉

TOP The clinical and tiny kitchen in the flat in Klosters. We needed more space so the painted armoire serves us well, while also providing a pretty addition to the white space. The small table hides the recycling, and the curtain is a Hungarian tablecloth. **RIGHT** In the opposite corner of the Shaker Heights kitchen we managed to reuse the original butler pantry of the house. The warm wood tone made it a special addition.

Living Rooms Are for Living, Not for Standing Around Politely

Living rooms, in all their forms, are a wonderful space to hang out—a place to relax, entertain, and bring your personality to life. Whether formal or casual, expansive or intimate, these spaces set the tone for how we live. Living rooms should invite everyone to linger and enjoy them fully, a philosophy shaped in part by my mother's flat in Hamburg. While endlessly cozy and welcoming when guests were over, the living and dining rooms were rarely used in our everyday lives. We congregated in the kitchen or retreated to our bedrooms, leaving these spaces feeling reserved and stiff.

Perhaps as a reaction to that stiffness, I've always sought to create living rooms that draw people in, places where formality doesn't sacrifice comfort. In our New Canaan home, we have three distinct sitting rooms: a formal living room, a library-turned-TV room, and a basement living room for the children. Each serves a purpose, and crucially, all are spaces we genuinely use.

A formal living room often acts as a "front-facing" room, setting the tone for the rest of the house. It's where you can display bold art, striking furniture, and carefully curated collections that might overwhelm in more casual spaces. It's also an opportunity to reflect the overall aesthetic of your home, pulling together elements of the art of the clash into one cohesive, inviting space.

Take the living room at Puddleduck Farm, for example. It features a proper bar–a centerpiece that encourages conversation and sets the stage for gatherings. Guests gravitate there first before spilling into the rest of the space. The room itself is layered with various seating spaces, thoughtfully curated art, and an effortless blend of traditional and contemporary design.

Contrast that with the adjoining family room, which Amanda describes as a space for lighting fires and lounging on oversized sofas. Where the formal living room impresses, the family room soothes–a wonderful example of how different sitting rooms can serve distinct purposes while complementing each other.

In Wolfgang and Hinrich's Hamburg home, the formal living room strikes a perfect balance between elegance and personality. Eclectic decor items lend

The living room in New Canaan. The walls are painted in Hellebore by Little Greene Paint. The fabric is my own design.

character, while the neoclassical wooden pillars on the other side of the room create a sense of grandeur. Yet, the sofas are deeply comfortable, inviting guests to sink in and stay awhile—a reminder that even the most formal spaces should prioritize comfort.

In Shaker Heights, the golden yellow walls of the formal living room gave the space a nice, glowing quality, while candle sconces and carefully spaced furniture enhanced the sense of intimacy. This larger room allowed for pieces to be spread out, creating pockets of interest while maintaining cohesion. Meanwhile, the TV room—a serene space adjoining the dining room with the same pale green walls—became the everyday heart of the house, a place where the family gathered to watch TV, read a book, craft, anything.

New Canaan's formal living room, though smaller, carries the spirit of the art of the clash. Rose pink walls, bold lighting choices, and contemporary art create a layered, visually arresting space. It's a room designed to make your eye travel, from the striking artwork to the patterns and textures that tie everything together.

The adjoining library, with its jewel-green walls and mustard yellow sofa, feels wonderfully snug. Despite the intense color palette, the room is softened by corner lamps that provide a warm, ambient glow. It's a space designed for quiet moments—reading, crafting, or simply unwinding.

Living rooms often need to serve multiple functions, particularly in homes with open plan designs or limited square footage. In Klosters, the living and dining areas share one space, making it essential to define distinct zones while maintaining a unified scheme. Clear boundaries, such as a rug or an artfully placed sofa, can delineate a living area within a larger room.

In New Canaan's basement, the living room doubles as a guest space, with a sofa bed providing additional sleeping quarters. The color scheme ties into the rest of the basement, creating continuity while ensuring the room feels cozy and welcoming.

A living room should be, as the name suggests, a room for living. I don't believe in the separation of family and living room. I understand the need for a space that is less formal, but I find it sad when you visit homes with living rooms that feel entirely lifeless. I believe every sitting room should feel comfortable and inviting. That starts with furniture—sofas and chairs that are as relaxing as they are stylish. Nothing is worse than beautiful furniture that no one wants to sit on. I remember vividly the chair that my mother loved but had such a stiff back and high seat that only a giant stick would have liked to sit on it. It was in her living room, of course, and despised by me and all of her close friends who knew to avoid it.

Layering is key to creating warmth and personality. Cushions, throws, and rugs add softness, while art and objects bring individuality. Large works of art can shine in a living room, providing a focal point that sets the mood for the space. Similarly, bold or unconventional furniture can find its home here—a sculptural coffee table or a brightly upholstered chair that adds a touch of the unexpected.

Lighting, too, plays a vital role. While well-placed recessed lights provide function, table and floor lamps create ambiance. In Shaker Heights, brass sconces and carefully placed lamps softened the golden hues of the living room, while in New Canaan, the library's corner lamps ensured the space felt snug without harshness.

The living room at Puddleduck Farm, a master class in the art of the clash.

TOP The family room in the flat in Klosters. It serves as a gathering place for the whole family and is as functional yet cozy as the small space could get. **RIGHT** The living room in our second house in Singapore. The gallery wall was born out of necessity as we couldn't take down the wooden entertainment accent wall. **NEXT PAGE** The living room of Hinrich and Wolfgang in Hamburg. Painted in the same pale yellow as the whole house, it nevertheless feels like its own distinct space.

A living room is the perfect canvas for expressing your personal style. It can be as formal or as relaxed as you like, as bold or as subdued. What matters is that it feels like yours—a space where you can entertain, unwind, and make memories. Whether it's a room dominated by contemporary art and bold patterns or a multi-functional space designed for both work and play, the living room should always invite you to live fully in it.

In the end, the art of the clash is about creating spaces that are uniquely yours. The living room, perhaps more than any other space, offers the opportunity to do just that. So let it reflect your life, your passions, and your personality—and don't be afraid to make it a little unexpected. After all, the best rooms are the ones that surprise and delight every time you step into them. ❖

TOP The library in New Canaan is one of the most used rooms in the house, after the kitchen. The jewel green shines especially in the evening when everyone wants to hang out. **BOTTOM** The living room window front in Shaker Heights. **OPPOSITE** The living room fireplace at Puddleduck Farm. The geometric art is a great counter to the classic architecture of the mantel. **NEXT PAGE** The family room at Puddleduck Farm used to be the sun porch and now serves as a wonderfully relaxed place to hang for the whole family.

The Dining Room Is a Chance to Play Dress Up

If the kitchen and living rooms are the heart and the facade of the home, the dining room is its elegant frock—an opportunity to dress up and make an impression. For some, the dining room is a cherished space for hosting and celebrating, while for others, it feels like an outdated relic. Yet, somewhere between the grand, formal dining rooms of the past and the casual, open-plan diners of modern homes lies a wonderful balance, where function meets personality and creativity.

The first step in designing a dining room is to consider how you'll use it. Do you love to host extravagant dinner parties? Is your kitchen too small for family meals, making the dining room essential for everyday dining? Or do you simply relish the idea of having a formal space for special occasions? The beauty of the dining room lies in its flexibility, allowing you to tailor it to your needs and desires. A dining room should never feel like a neglected showpiece—it should invite you in and be a space you love to use.

Our dining room in New Canaan is the largest room in the house and also serves as my studio, blending practicality with beauty. Slightly apart from the main living areas, it's located above the garage, with a few steps leading down into the space. The brick fireplace is a focal point and during the colder months, I often light a fire while I work, adding warmth and comfort to the room.

The size of the room allows for bold, large-scale elements. Two brass pendants (repurposed from our Shaker Heights kitchen) hang overhead, while the centerpiece is a large oak dining table that previously served as my office desk. A striking watercolor portrait watches over the space from above the fireplace, and postmodern dining chairs—painted a rich orange-brown and upholstered in colorful fabric—add personality. The room is rounded off with a dark green ceiling and window nooks, contrasting beautifully with the crisp white slanted walls. My desk is positioned by the window, a favorite spot to work.

In stark contrast, the dining area in Klosters is part of the living room. The small table and red chairs echo the flat's overall color scheme, while the painted credenza is a nod to regional craftsmanship. The space is intimate and practical, offering a different kind of charm. Though small, it perfectly reflects the peaceful atmosphere of the entire flat.

BROMLEY

PREVIOUS PAGE The dining room at Puddleduck Farm. The green lacquered walls are a stroke of genius on the low room as the reflection of the light makes it feel light yet very cozy. The table is made of one slab of wood set on heavy plexiglass feet, the Hugo dining chairs are upholstered in a blue wool fabric, and the window treatments are Schumacher's "Chiang Mai Dragon." **TOP AND RIGHT** The dining room of Hinrich and Wolfgang in Hamburg is painted the same pale yellow as the rest of the house. The table linens and pillows are "La Vie en Rose" from my own textile line.

Amanda's green lacquered dining room at Puddleduck Farm is a showstopper that balances bold design with functionality, proving that elegance doesn't have to come at the expense of comfort. The walls, finished in a rich lacquer, are bold yet inviting, setting the stage for memorable dinners. The centerpiece is an incredible dining table made from a single slab of wood supported by plexiglass legs, paired with mid-century modern chairs. Contemporary artwork and vibrant window treatments with patterned fabrics add to the drama and sophistication. Despite its grandeur, the room feels anything but stiff. During dinner parties, the lacquered walls reflect the warm glow of brass sconces and Amanda's signature abundance of candles, creating a magical, dynamic atmosphere. The old house has slightly wonky floors that add to the feeling of being in an extraordinary space.

IVY
IVY

Wolfgang and Hinrich's dining room leans more formal but is softened by their incredible hosting skills. Anchored by a Chinese screen mounted high above the sideboard, the room draws the eye upward, lending a sense of grandeur. The large mahogany dining table reinforces the classic feel, yet their collection of Barbie dolls dressed as drag queens perched on the windowsills adds a playful, unexpected twist. This juxtaposition keeps the space from feeling overly serious, making it uniquely theirs.

The dining room in Shaker Heights was a well-loved space. Pale green paneled walls provided a serene backdrop, and the sleek modern dining table complemented the room's simplicity. While it lacked the layering I now prioritize—window treatments and a rug would have pulled everything together—it remained a beautiful and functional space for family meals and gatherings.

Dining rooms offer unique opportunities for creative expression, perhaps more than any other room in the house. They can be as formal or as casual as you like, as multifunctional or as single purpose as you need. Ultimately, the dining room should reflect your lifestyle and personality. It's a space to gather, celebrate, and create memories—but only if you let it be one. The key is to follow what makes you happy, embracing both tradition and innovation to craft a space that feels uniquely yours. ❖

FAR LEFT The dining room in our first condo in Singapore. LEFT AND BOTTOM The dining room in Shaker Heights. The original panelled walls were painted in Ball Green by Farrow & Ball. NEXT PAGE The family room that also serves as the dining room in the flat in Klosters during the winter months, while the terrace beyond serves as an outdoor dining room during the warmer months.

Interlude
IVY
Rosé

Be Your Own Best Guest

Let me tell you a little secret: I'm not much for the overblown fuss that often accompanies "hosting" these days. Yes, I love to cook and I'm fairly good at it. Yes, I enjoy creating beautiful, inviting tables. But what I excel at, and what I truly love, is bringing people together. Because a great gathering always starts with the people. My goal is to leave you with the confidence that when you assemble that perfect mix of personalities, the atmosphere will be exactly as it should—joyful, warm, and memorable.

Before we dive into creating the perfect atmosphere, let me tell you a story. It's about hosting, cooking, and throwing a dinner party—though it isn't my story, but my parents'. My parents, who were, for a time, the most fabulous hosts I've ever known (despite their marriage, like my mother, now being gone).

In the late 1970s, my parents were just married, living in Paris. My father had been there for a while, and my mother had joined him from Munich, barely speaking any French and knowing no one besides my father. Determined to make an impression, she planned a dinner party, inviting a mix of his friends—many of whom, according to family lore, were his ex-lovers.

With her Bavarian sensibilities and a steely resolve, my mother bought a substantial pork roast in her halting French and prepared it as she had learned growing up: Schweinsbraten mit Knödel (roast pork with Bavarian dumplings). It's a dish I have never attempted in my life and never will—yet Mami found it just the right thing to serve for her first dinner party in Paris. Their kitchen, in a then-gritty corner of the 17th arrondissement, was tiny, but she persevered.

The guests were invited for 8 p.m. By 8:30, no one had arrived. (Anyone familiar with Parisian culture knows what's coming.) By 9, still no guests. The roast had dried to the consistency of shoe leather, the dumplings had dissolved into chewy mush, the kitchen was thick with smoke, and my mother was a hot mess who was calming her nerves with heaps of wine.

Finally, guests began to trickle in, at a normal Parisian dinner time (I assume 9:30 to 10 p.m.). My father dashed to the local brasserie to buy oysters. Windows were thrown open and food smoke replaced with cigarette smoke. My mother's French became fluent for the first time, aided by "ALL THAT VINE," and she simply

embraced the chaos. By the early hours of the morning, the dinner party had become a roaring success—a story of laughter and resilience that would go down in family lore.

Why do I tell you this story? First, because I love it. My mother was a legendary hostess, not because her food was always perfect (though she was a good cook), or because her table settings were impeccable (though they often were). No, her magic lay in the atmosphere she created. It was all about the feeling—the raucous laughter, the heated debates, the sense of connection.

That night in Paris taught her an important lesson, one she never tired of repeating to me: Be your own best guest.

This philosophy is at the heart of the art of the clash. Hosting, and by extension creating a home, isn't about perfection—it's about creating an environment where you, your family, and your friends feel at ease; where conversation flows; and where you, the host, are as much a part of the fun as your guests.

Of course, a great group of people can be enhanced by the right atmosphere—or hindered by the wrong one. But the food, the decor, the lighting—these are tools to support the gathering, not the focus of it. This is where your role truly shines; your guests will take their cue from you.

IVY

MÖBEL

TOP LEFT Wolfgang and Hinrich, in their element as the complete hosts they are. BOTTOM RIGHT My very dapper Papi, presenting one of my pillows.

If you're relaxed, joyful, and engaged, they will be too. A beautifully laid table or a perfectly executed meal is no substitute for the energy and warmth you bring to the room.

Like every other aspect of the art of the clash, hosting is about finding joy in contrasts. It's in the balance of effort and ease, planning and spontaneity. It's in embracing the unexpected, whether it's a dinner gone awry or an unplanned late-night singalong.

So, as you prepare to host your next gathering, take a page from my mother's book. Bring your people together, create an atmosphere of warmth and connection, and most importantly, enjoy the party as much as they do. Let's all be more like her—fluent in fun, fueled by good wine, and forever the life of the party. Be your own best guest. Yet another perfect quip from my ever-present Mami. ❖

IVY

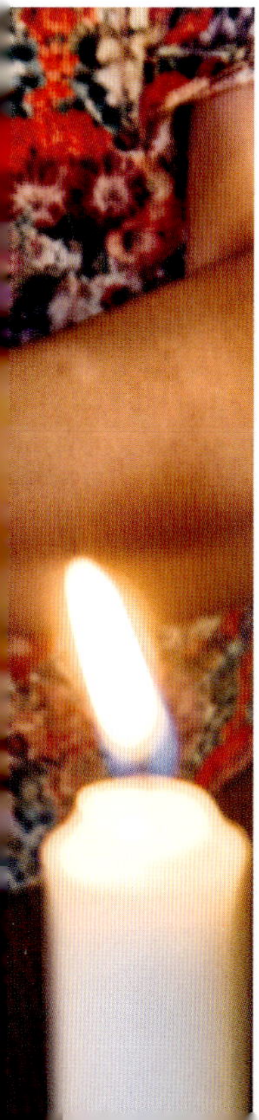

Bedrooms as the Heart of Comfort and Personal Expression

Bedrooms, whether they belong to you, your children, or your guests, are the most personal spaces in a home. They invite comfort, offer a retreat, and are often the rooms where individuality can shine brightest. As the coziest corners of the house, bedrooms are a canvas for creativity—places where texture, color, and personal touches combine to create a deeply inviting atmosphere.

In many homes, the primary bedroom revolves around the bed, the largest and most prominent piece of furniture in the room. This centerpiece provides endless opportunities for creativity, from headboards to nightstands and lighting. In our New Canaan home, the bed has a canopy—a feature I had dreamed of for as long as I can remember. The room's elongated proportions make the canopy bed an ideal anchor, giving structure to the space.

The curtains, in one of my original textile designs and reused from our Shaker Heights home, span nearly the entire length of the opposite wall, softening the room and enhancing its symmetry. For the walls, I chose a warm beige-brown and extended the paint to the ceiling, creating a monochromatic cocoon that serves as a versatile backdrop for layering textures and colors. Red nightstands and lamps, paired with an orange chest of drawers and touches of blue, add personality while tying the room together with the patterned rug and curtains.

Amanda's guest bedroom at Puddleduck Farm employs a similar palette. A bespoke headboard designed by Amanda wraps the bed on the wall side, creating an enveloping feel. Across the room, modern built-ins with curved edges contrast beautifully with an antique chair and contemporary lighting. This masterful combination of old and new is a hallmark of the art of the clash, proving that eclectic elements can feel cohesive when approached thoughtfully.

Our master bedroom in Shaker Heights took a completely different direction. Dark blue walls echoed the deep tones in the curtains, creating a rich and dramatic setting. The rattan headboard—originally purchased in Singapore—showcased the region's extraordinary craftsmanship and brought a sense of warmth to the space.

FISKE GUIDE
COLLEGES

Andrea Camilleri
MEG HOWREY
THEY'RE GOING TO LOVE YOU
Jojo Moyes
The Giver of Stars
ALICE HOFFMAN
THE RULES OF MAGIC
Keller Züricher Novellen

PREVIOUS PAGE The teenage daughter's bedroom at Puddleduck Farm. As with many of Amanda's designs, patterns have been expertly mixed creating a cohesive scheme. The wallpaper is Fanned Fronds by Anthropologie. **LEFT AND TOP** The primary bedroom in New Canaan. The shelving unit is from IKEA. The curtains are my own designs, spanning almost the whole wall to add some balance to the space. The red lamps were made to order from oversized vases.

To counterbalance the moody blues, we introduced bold artwork: an abstract oil painting in shades of orange and red and a large scarf with a design reminiscent of Gauguin's vibrant palettes forms.

In contrast, the guest bedroom in Shaker Heights was cooler and more serene. Rose pink walls, mustard yellow trim, and a matching yellow reading nook by the window created an inviting, whimsical space. A floral print from my first collection added a delicate touch, tying the elements together with subtlety and charm.

Designing children's bedrooms presents a unique challenge: creating spaces that delight in the moment but can also grow with their inhabitants. In Shaker Heights, our daughter's room was a four-year-old's dream. Pink walls, floral textiles, and a plush bed made it a space she loved to spend time in, a testament to the room's success.

In New Canaan, her bedroom has taken on a more mature feel while still accommodating her current needs. Though the foundational pieces of furniture remain the same, the larger space allowed for the addition of a chest of drawers. A happy green for her walls, yellow and pink window treatments—another of my original textile designs—and

THIS PAGE AND OPPOSITE Our daughter's green bedroom in New Canaan. I've used most of the same furniture as in Shaker Heights but the green walls as well as the window treatment make it feel like a very different room. **FOLLOWING** Our son's blue bedroom in New Canaan. Having art that he could let his eyes wander over was one of his requests, as well as the wall color. His bed has been handed down in my family and originally belonged to my great-grandmother, while the antique quilt in the Lone Star pattern hails from Texas.

thoughtfully chosen artwork give the room a timeless quality, ensuring it will evolve beautifully as she grows.

Our son's New Canaan bedroom, painted in Farrow & Ball's Stone Blue, reflects his own personality. A thrifted striped fabric works seamlessly with the walls, creating a boy-like but still warm and inviting atmosphere. The centerpiece of the room is a cherished desk inherited from my father—a piece imbued with sentimental value and history. This connection feels fitting, as my son shares many traits with his grandfather. A good array of choices from our art collection allow him to let his eyes wander, something he was adamant to achieve.

At Puddleduck Farm, Amanda's two teenager's bedrooms are a testament to creating spaces that grow with their inhabitants. The green room for her daughter features striking wallpaper, mid-century modern furniture, and pops of color, while in her son's bedroom, the gray walls employ a subtler palette without losing warmth or charm. Both rooms strike a perfect balance between sophistication and playfulness, ensuring they remain welcoming whether the kids are studying, sleeping, or hanging out with friends.

ALL THAT DREAMS MATTERS

In Wolfgang and Hinrich's Hamburg home, their master bedroom showcases their signature boldness. A large oil portrait anchors the room, complemented by an antique Japanese silk kimono displayed above the bed. The vibrant citron yellow walls envelop the space in warmth and energy, while a vintage real tiger rug adds an exotic, unique touch that only their home could carry off.

One thing you'll notice across all these bedrooms is the absence of matching furniture sets. Before moving to the U.S., I had never encountered the concept, and while I can understand the practicality, I've always found them aesthetically limiting. Even in a home with a traditional style, piecing together complementary furniture allows for greater depth and personality than a uniform set ever could.

In a bedroom, individuality is key. It's a space for rest and reflection, but also one where your personal style can take center stage. A blend of pieces—perhaps a vintage bedside table paired with a modern upholstered headboard—creates a sense of history and story, making the space feel truly lived-in and loved.

Ultimately, bedrooms should always prioritize comfort, no matter who is settling down in them. They're deeply personal spaces, and while they offer endless opportunities for creative expression, their primary goal is to make you feel at ease. The best bedrooms are those that reflect your personality, tell a story, and, most importantly, make your heart sing. ❖

OPPOSITE The guest room in Shaker Heights. **LEFT** The bedroom of the teenage son at Puddleduck Farm. **BOTTOM** The guest room in New Canaan. The space is very small so I leaned into the feeling of coziness by painting the ceiling in the same color and keeping colors in a similar palette.

The unexpected pop of colors make these three bedrooms more interesting: the bright blue Chippendale chair and pleated lampshade in the primary bedroom in New Canaan (OPPOSITE), the gradient blue curtain in the guest bedroom at Puddleduck Farm (TOP), and the bright orange artwork in the primary bedroom in Shaker Heights (BOTTOM).

TOP The built-in vanity desk was constructed after Amanda's designs and made especially for the guest bedroom at Puddleduck Farm. RIGHT The green guest room at Puddleduck Farm works well with a daybed in the small space in lieu of a full bed. NEXT PAGE The primary bedroom at Hinrich and Wolfgang's Hamburg house is as grand as the rest of the house. A large oil painting of Hinrich dominates the well-balanced space.

CARY GRANT
An Affair to Remember
CARY GRANT
CARY GRANT
CARY GRANT

Hallways, Entryways, Bathrooms, and Other Spaces that Connect

What makes a home feel cohesive? The answer often lies in the spaces that connect—the hallways, entryways, mudrooms, and bathrooms that stitch a house together. While these areas might seem secondary, they have the power to set the tone for the entire home. These in-between spaces offer an opportunity to extend your style, introduce unexpected elements, and make a house feel not only intentional but also a true reflection of its inhabitants.

A well-designed entry hall can create an unforgettable first impression. Wolfgang and Hinrich's grand entryway in Hamburg is a striking example. Minimalistic compared to the rest of their home, it features carefully selected contemporary art and African statues that serve as a prelude to the bold and eclectic interiors beyond. The adjoining hallways and staircase continue this theme, with large-scale artworks that dominate the space, adding drama and intrigue. Their ability to embrace bombastic pieces ensures that these transitional areas feel just as intentional as the living spaces.

At Puddleduck Farm, Amanda's entry hall offers a very different kind of welcome. Built in the 1700s, the airy, open layout is surprising but not unwelcome. Steps lead down to the living room on one side, while the dining room and library beckon on the other. Amanda's impeccable taste is evident in the details: a beautiful kilim rug, an antique statue, and thoughtful placement of decor and furniture. The space feels light, inviting, and deeply connected to the rest of the home.

In contrast, the entry hall in our New Canaan house is all about boldness. A striking color palette, an oversized work of art, and layered textures define the space. A wicker pendant light softens the edges, while a brass table lamp atop a mid-century modern side table provides warmth. Together, these elements set the tone for the house, creating a dynamic tension between modern and traditional.

Even in smaller spaces, an entry hall can make an impact. In our Klosters flat, the compact entryway encapsulates the art of the clash. An antique painted trunk juxtaposed with oversized contemporary art and two terracotta table lamps creates a sense of balance and intrigue. The tone is clear: this is not your typical Alpine

PREVIOUS PAGE The entry hall at Puddleduck Farm. The wallpaper in the staircase is from Cole & Son. **OPPOSITE** The small hallway leading to the mudroom in Shaker Heights. I painted a mural that was originally inspired by our garden in Singapore but eventually became just nature inspired. I never got to finish it but thoroughly enjoyed the experience.

chalet-style apartment but a space that nods to the region while staying surprising and very much ours.

Hallways often get overlooked, yet they offer a prime canvas for creativity. Large-scale art and furniture are one of my favorite ways to add personality and style to these connecting spaces. In New Canaan, the downstairs hallway features artwork with strong lines that draw the eye and create visual interest. The mudroom allows for the oversized trunk from the 1700s to stand out. Playing with scale in these areas ensures they leave an impression, setting the tone for the rooms beyond.

Amanda's use of wallpaper in the staircase at Puddleduck Farm demonstrates the power of pattern and color. The playfulness of her choices breathes life into what could easily be a forgettable space, creating a transition that feels as intentional as the main rooms of the house.

Bathrooms and powder rooms may be the last spaces you tackle in a renovation, but they hold immense potential for creativity. These often utilitarian areas can become luxurious retreats or unique design moments that leave a lasting impression, even without a full renovation.

At Puddleduck Farm, Amanda's upstairs bathroom shows how even small updates can transform a space with a bold wallpaper and a pretty shower curtain elevating the room. The powder room is another standout, with Clarence House Tibet wallpaper offset by a navy trim and ceiling. Amanda's fearless approach to layering color, pattern, and even a collection of rubber ducks makes the space both memorable and inviting.

TOP LEFT The powder room at Puddleduck Farm, which Amanda wallpapered in Cole & Son's Tibet wallpaper. TOP RIGHT The basement powder room in New Canaan. The walls are painted in Hick's Blue by Little Greene Paint. OPPOSITE The bathroom at Puddleduck Farm, with another great choice of wallpaper called Acquario Ink by Cole & Son.

In Shaker Heights, our powder room was equally striking. Red gloss walls paired with a Peranakan-style wash bowl created a dramatic effect, while a mural in the adjacent hallway—depicting our Singapore garden—offered a vibrant contrast. The interplay of colors and patterns turned these small spaces into unexpected focal points.

The basement bathroom in New Canaan was more of an improvised project but turned out surprisingly well. Budget constraints led me to an outlet for tiles, resulting in dark red wall tiling and unusual floor tiles. A leftover can of dark blue paint helped pull the colors together and provide depth, while an old pine dresser repurposed as a vanity brought character. Using matching fabric for the shower curtain and toilet room vanity curtain tied the spaces together, creating a sense of cohesion.

What ties all these examples together is their ability to reflect the personality of the home while maintaining a cohesive design. These connecting spaces are like the side dishes at Thanksgiving: often overshadowed by the main course but essential to the overall experience. A hallway leading to a kitchen or a staircase connecting levels are

LEFT The guest bathroom in New Canaan. The sconces are from Pooky Lights, with lampshades Geraldine of my own design.
TOP The guest bathroom in Shaker Heights. We cut into the original pine closet to create the space for the vanities and installed a free-standing bathtub.

opportunities to create continuity, bridging the bold statements of one room with the quiet elegance of another.

Ultimately, the spaces that connect a house are more than just functional; they're an integral part of its story. Whether it's a hallway with a gallery-like collection of art, a mudroom that boasts both practicality and style, or a powder room that surprises with its boldness, these areas deserve as much attention as the main rooms.

The beauty of the art of the clash is that it embraces every corner of a home, finding potential in the spaces that might otherwise be overlooked. By treating these transitional areas as opportunities for creativity, you ensure that your home doesn't just look cohesive, it feels cohesive—a seamless blend of style and substance that truly makes it your own. ❖

Three spaces from Shaker Heights: the entry hall with the hallway leading to the kitchen (TOP), the office space in the attic (BOTTOM), and finally the enfilade view from the hallway toward our daughter's bedroom (OPPOSITE). NEXT PAGE View from the entry hall toward the living room at Puddleduck Farm.

TOP The blue mudroom in Shaker Heights. Having a sink in the mudroom was one of the most practical things and used regularly. **BOTTOM** A corner of the entry hall in New Canaan, with a view toward the living room. The pink artwork is by the Guerilla Girls. **OPPOSITE** The basement hallway toward the garden in Hinrich and Wolfgang's townhouse in Hamburg. Painted in a warmer yellow than the rest of the house, everything is oversized in the small and low space. Paired with the black-and-white checker floor, it makes for a striking effect.

LEFT The staircase at Puddleduck Farm. The black-and-white photograph lends a great contrast to the geometric wallpaper and is a great example of how much the spaces between can add to the feeling of a home. **RIGHT** The mudroom in New Canaan that came about more as an afterthought but has proven very useful. The pillows on the bamboo bench are from my own line.

Conclusion

MERRY
CHRISTMAS

YOU ARE LEAVING
THE
AMERICAN SECTOR
SIE VERLASSEN DEN
AMERIKANISCHEN
SEKTOR
US ARMY

A Manifesto Against Mundane Design

Perhaps this is a little philosophical, but I believe the human experience is as beautiful as it is messy precisely because of its glorious imperfections. Life, in all its chaos, has a richness and complexity that makes it extraordinary. And so should your home.

This final chapter is an opportunity to delve into what I call A Manifesto Against Mundane Design. Don't get me wrong—I think there is immense beauty in the mundane, which literally means "day-to-day." But somewhere along the way, the word took on a new connotation: something bland, devoid of meaning or intention. And that's where the trouble begins.

For me, the mundane in interiors is epitomized by a lack of personality. It is homes styled entirely with Restoration Hardware catalogues. It's boxy, misunderstood attempts at Bauhaus-inspired architecture that dominate the landscape of new builds. It is spaces designed not for the people living in them but for the approval of others. In short, it's the opposite of the art of the clash.

Let me clarify: I understand the desire to please others. I care about what people think—probably less than I did when I was younger, but the impulse is still there. Yet I've found that when I create something that feels 100% like *me*, that worry fades away. If a space brings me joy, why should it matter whether someone else approves?

This mindset is something I inherited from my mother. She was a curious blend of attention seeking and devil-may-care, but she taught me one of the most valuable lessons I've ever learned: *you are your own closest friend.* If you love something—truly love it—it radiates outward and draws people in. This philosophy guided her in everything she did, from hosting to decorating to moving to a new city at the not so young age of sixty-five.

And so it should be with your interiors. Your home should feel like a warm embrace, a space that reflects who you are and what you love.

What I find most disheartening in many modern interiors is the loss of personality. The idea that you can step into a space and immediately understand who lives there has become a rarity. Too often, homes feel like showrooms—polished, impersonal, and devoid of soul.

Contrast this with homes that are unapologetically personal. Puddleduck Farm, for instance, is a masterpiece of warmth and individuality. It's a little rambling, very elegant yet effortlessly lived-in without feeling cluttered, and brimming with character. Amanda's style is immediately apparent—it's worldly, layered, and utterly inviting. It's the kind of place you want to linger, just as you want to linger in the company of Amanda and her family.

Hinrich and Wolfgang's Hamburg townhouse exudes a similar spirit. Their collections are unparalleled, but it's their hospitality that truly shines. Their home feels like an extension of their personalities—filled with treasures, memories, and quirks that make it uniquely theirs. They're the kind of hosts who make you feel utterly at ease, as though their home was made just for you, even while it's so clearly made for them.

This is what I strive for in my own home in New Canaan. I want it to be welcoming to everyone who steps through the door, but more importantly, I want it to feel like home for *us*. Because that is the goal of the art of the clash: creating a house that feels uniquely yours, one step at a time.

Our New Canaan home is a reflection of the lessons I've learned by designing and living in other places. It's a space that prioritizes comfort without sacrificing style, filled with pieces that tell a story. The oversized artwork in the entry hall, the kitchen that forgoes upper cabinets in favor of light and airiness, the rose-pink living room—every decision was made with intention.

This doesn't mean every choice has to be bold or unconventional. Sometimes it's the smallest, most personal details that make the biggest impact: a well-loved chair inherited from family, a collection of mismatched

WATTEAU
DIE GEMÄLDESAMMLUNG DES
LOUVRE
Lawrence Gowing
monte
Zeitgenössische Kunst in der Deutschen Bank
WIENER WERKSTÄTTE
Flammarion
BRANCUSI
Toulouse-Lautrec
18
62.

plates from travels, or a piece of art that speaks to your soul. These are the touches that transform a house into a home.

What ties all of this together—whether it's the homes of friends or my own—is the rejection of the mundane. It's a celebration of the beautiful mess of life, with all its quirks, imperfections, and individuality. The art of the clash is about embracing that mess, letting it guide your creativity, and crafting spaces that reflect your unique story.

So let this be your manifesto against the mundane. Design your home for yourself, not for the expectations of others. Fill it with pieces you love, colors that make your heart sing, and objects that tell your story. Let it be imperfect, layered, and alive. Because in the end, your home is not just a space to live—it's an extension of who you are.

And that is the essence of the art of the clash: a home that feels like *you*. ❖

Acknowledgments

First, I want to thank my editor, Juree Sondker, and the whole team at Gibbs Smith for giving me a chance and seeing the vision I so truly believe in. Their excitement and joy for this project carried me along throughout the creation process and made me believe in myself. Thank you!

I also want to thank Andrea Ceraso who photographed most of the projects in the book. Her eye and incredible work ethic made a very tight timeline possible—plus she is a hilarious travel companion. I can't wait to shoot more projects together in the future!

Ellie McNevin: thank you for planting the seed of the idea of this book, for connecting me to Juree, and for helping me get it over the threshold. This whole thing would not have happened without you! To you and your great team at the Birdie Agency, thank you.

To Amanda and Barney, my wonderful friends and owners of Puddleduck: thank you for letting me follow through on this crazy idea. Barney, thank you for giving up your house and space for me. And Amanda, thank you for your friendship, for your inspiring eye, for your wonderful sense of humor—and for that green lacquered dining room that needs to go down in design history.

To Hinrich and Wolfgang, my dearest friends. You initially were Mami's friends when I met you at the young age of sixteen. You were so important to her, and have become just as important for me, for us. Thank you for allowing me to be the one who gets to show the world what an incredible home you have built. I treasure this more than words can describe.

To Pina and Mario: Thank you for incredible hard work on our New Canaan house. Your enthusiasm, dedication, and friendship made this a wonderful collaboration with many more to come.

Dawn Cook, my mentor and inspiration to go more deeply into design, I thank you. I wouldn't have dared without your encouragement.

To my OGs: you know who you are. Thank you for your eternal and best friendships.

Steff, the Klosters photo shoot wouldn't have been possible without your help! And I wouldn't be who I am without you as my friend. Thank you.

To Noemi: thank you for being the force that you are and holding down the fort at SWD while I was knee-deep in this project. Your support means everything, and I am so lucky to have you as a partner and friend.

Thank you, Papi and Marion, for your support in every moment. Your pride in my work means a lot to me and encourages me to continue.

To my husband and my three beloved children: Danke. Ich liebe Euch aus vollem Herzen. Thank you for being as excited about this and about the houses as I am. Thank you for going along with my crazy ideas. I wouldn't be here without you.

And finally, to my beloved Mamilein: thank you for the crazy, unconventional, often-hard-but-always-laughter-filled upbringing. I would not be who I am without having you as my mother. I miss you. ❖

Photo Credits

Andrea Ceraso: Cover front and back, 2–3, 4, 7–8, 11, 12 top left, 12 top right, 12 bottom right, 13 top, 14, 16–17, 19, 25, 26–27, 30 top, 31, 32, 33 top, 35, 37 top left and top right, 38 top left, 40, 41, 43, 46, 47 top left and top right, 48 top, 49, 50–51, 53, 54 top, 55, 56, 57 top and bottom left, 58 top left and top right, 59, 60–61, 64, 68 top and bottom, 69 top, 70 top, 71, 75, 76, 77, 78 top left, 78 top right, 79, 80–81, 83, 84, 85, 86, 87, 88 top and bottom, 89, 90, 95, 96, 97, 100, 103, 104–5, 106, 107, 109, 110–11, 112 top right, 115, 116, 117 top, 118–19, 120, 121, 122, 123 bottom, 124–25, 129, 130, 131 top, 134 top, 135, 138, 141, 142, 143 top, 145, 146 top, 148–49, 150 top, 151, 152–53, 155, 156–57, 162–63, 175, 176–77, 178, 179 top, 180 top and bottom, 181 top, 182–83, 185 top and bottom, 186, 187 top, 188–89, 190–91, 193, 194–95, 198 top left and top right, 199, 200, 203–4, 206 bottom, 207, 208, 209, 210–11, 212, 215, 216, 217 top, 218

Anna-Lena Ehlers: 22 bottom middle, 23, 158, 159, 164–65, 166, 168, 169, 170–71, 172–73, 222–23

Bram Laebens: 6–7, 22 bottom left, 99 top and bottom
Claire Morin: 12 bottom left, 36, 38 bottom left, 58 bottom right, 112 top left, 206 top

Sharon Hughes: 18 top, 22–23 top left, 28, 34, 38 top right, 38 bottom right, 39 top, 42, 45, 52, 57 bottom right, 58 bottom left, 62, 65, 66 top, 67, 72–73, 91, 92–93, 101 top, 102, 112 bottom left and bottom right, 113 top, 123 top, 132 top, 133, 137, 139, 150 bottom, 161 top, 162 bottom, 184 top, 187 bottom, 196, 201 top, 202 top and bottom, 203

Sven C. Raben: 114

Painting by Pierre-Auguste Renoir, *Romaine Lacaux*, 1864. The Cleveland Museum of Art, gift of the Hanna Fund, p. 30 bottom

From the private archive of Sophie von Oertzen Williamson: 29 top, 82 top, 98 top, 147, 160 top, 214 top

About the Author

Sophie von Oertzen Williamson is the creative force behind Sophie Williamson Design, a design studio rooted in color, storytelling, and a fearless embrace of contrast. Her designs are defined by a layered, collected aesthetic that balances boldness with beauty and that feel deeply personal, considered, and full of life.

Born in Switzerland to German parents and raised between Switzerland, Germany, and the UK, Sophie's design eye was shaped early on by an appreciation for the eclectic, the imperfect, and the richly textured. Her journey to design was far from linear. Before founding her studio, she lived all over Europe as well as Singapore and then Shaker Heights, Ohio, collecting inspiration and developing a visual language that speaks to the joyful tension of opposites.

It was during her time in Singapore—amid the vibrant chaos of colors, cultures, and styles—that Sophie first began to understand her own creativity. What began as a love for setting a table and decorating evolved into a more formal practice with the launch of her own collection of illustrated table linens and soft furnishings.

Her signature style celebrates the interplay of color, pattern, scale, and era. It is a practice grounded in instinct but refined through experience. Her rooms might include eighteenth-century antiques alongside contemporary art, or an inherited trunk paired with a bright modern rug—but they always feel like they belong.

Now based in Connecticut with her Anglo-Belgian husband and three children, Sophie runs her home decor business and is slowly taking on clients for interior design. She is also the voice behind *Sophie Says*, a Substack publication where she shares thoughts on interiors, taste, hosting, and the ongoing adventure of building a creative life.

Above all, Sophie believes a home should feel lived in, loved, and unmistakably yours. Hers is a manifesto against the mundane—a design practice that champions joy, memory, and the beauty of the beautifully imperfect. ❖

First Edition
30 29 28 27 26 5 4 3 2 1

Published by
Gibbs Smith
570 N. Sportsplex Drive
Kaysville, Utah 84037
www.gibbs-smith.com
The authorized representative in the EEA is Simon and Schuster Netherlands BV, Herculesplein 96 3584 AA Utrecht, Netherlands, info@simonandschuster.nl

Designed by The Sly Studio
Art director: Ryan Thomann
Editor: Juree Sondker
Production manager: Felix Gregorio

Printed and bound in China

Library of Congress Control Number: 2025938812
ISBN: 978-1-4236-6856-5

This product is made of FSC®-certified and other controlled material.